Show Me!

Graphic Organizers for Reading Comprehension across the Curriculum

- Set a purpose for reading
- Preview and predict
- Make inferences
- Analyze cause and effect
- Identify facts and opinions
- Draw conclusions
- Use context clues

Katherine Scraper
Vickie L. Scraper

Good Year Books
Tucson, Arizona

Good Year Books

Our titles are available for most basic curriculum subjects plus many enrichment areas. For more Good Year Books, contact your local bookseller or educational dealer. For a complete catalog with information about other Good Year Books, please contact:

Good Year Books
PO Box 91858
Tucson, AZ 85752-1858
www.goodyearbooks.com

Library of Congress Cataloging-in-Publication Data
Scraper, Katherine
    Show me! : graphic organizers for reading comprehension across the curriculum/
    Katherine Scraper, Vickie L. Scraper
        p. cm.
    ISBN-13: 978-1-59647-092-7
    ISBN-10: 1-59647-092-5
    1. Reading comprehension--Study and teaching (Elementary)
    2. Reading (Elementary)--Audio-visual aids. I. Scraper, Vickie L. II. Title.

LB1573.7.S38 2006
372.47--dc22

2006043519

Cover Design: Gary D. Smith, Performance Design
Text Design: Doug Goewey
Photo on page 76 by Takver, courtesy Wikipedia.com
Drawings on page 199: "pulling my leg" by Ken Shinzato,
                "letting the cat out of the bag" and "on cloud nine" by Torylin Crowe

ISBN-10: 1-59647-092-5
ISBN-13: 978-1-59647-092-7

1 2 3 4 5 6 7 8 9 ML 13 12 11 10 09 08 07 06

Preface

A survey of educational journals and Web sites reveals literally thousands of articles on the benefits of using graphic organizers to enhance reading comprehension in all genres and content areas. We quickly learn that using graphic organizers helps students:

- tackle information head-on and connect what they already know with what they learn

- develop vocabulary

- prioritize, categorize, and summarize information

- visually represent their ideas, leading to improved comprehension and retention of key concepts.

How did this particular book come about, though?

Fact #1: Teachers nationwide are responsible for teaching strategies to prepare students for state reading assessments—and, more importantly, for success as life-long readers.

Fact #2: Graphic organizers help promote familiarity and mastery of these strategies by asking students to "show" their thinking processes.

Fact #3: Students benefit when teachers have quality resources at their disposal.

Conclusion: Teachers + *Show Me! Graphic Organizers for Reading Comprehension Across the Curriculum* = students who better relate to, understand, and remember what they read.

In short, we wrote *Show Me!* to use in our own classrooms. Although many graphic organizers are available in the current educational market, we and our colleagues saw a need for a resource book that:

- addresses required fiction, nonfiction, and word-study reading strategies;

- organizes the Table of Contents by reading strategy rather than subject area or graphic organizer type;

- includes reading strategy descriptions;

- includes explicit lessons for teaching the reading strategies to students;

- includes reading selections that incorporate the strategies with accompanying completed graphic organizers to use as models;

- includes graphic organizer blackline masters that aren't "fussy" and, once learned, can easily be replicated by students to utilize during classroom assignments, independent reading, and testing situations;

- emphasizes the reciprocity of reading and writing by having students use the graphic organizer as a writing planner;

- includes extension activities to help teachers address reading strategies throughout the school day and help students learn to generalize and apply the strategies to new texts and situations; and

- includes an assessment piece to monitor students' strategy acquisition and follow-up.

Following are examples of experts' observations regarding the use of graphic organizers for reading comprehension:

- *Graphic organizers . . . have been widely researched for their effectiveness in improving learning outcomes for various students. . . . Although reading is by far the most well studied application, science, social studies, language arts, and math are additional content areas that are represented in the research base on graphic organizers.*

Tracey Hall and Nicole Strangmen, "Graphic Organizers," National Center on Accessing the General Curriculum, 2002

- *The use of graphic organizers can help students link existing knowledge organized in schemas to new knowledge, thereby increasing their understanding. . . . The use of graphic organizers jump-starts the flow of thoughts and words.*

  Nancy Mowat, "Effective Use of Visual Learning Tools to Improve Student Learning . . . and More!" *Multimedia & Internet @ Schools*, March 2004

- *In a concrete way, utilizing graphic organizers is an inexpensive literacy dynamic that taps into prior knowledge, cultivates active participation, and fosters an understanding of conceptual relationships, leading to a facilitation of comprehension.*

  Courtney P. Millet, "Graphic Organizers: An Integral Component to Facilitate Comprehension During Basal Reading Instruction," *Reading Improvement*, December 2000

- *Graphic organizers have been found to be effective in teaching technical vocabulary, helping students organize what they are learning, and improving recall of information. . . . The graphic organizer is tailored to current theory regarding how the brain processes information and has been found effective in learning general vocabulary.*

  Michelle P. Orme, "Developing Mathematical Vocabulary," *Preventing School Failure*, March 2002

- *The visual representation of information is also a strong tradition in the social studies, which draws heavily on the use of maps, globes, charts, and tables. Another form of visual presentation, the graphic organizer, has received attention recently as an effective way to help students understand content. . . .*

  Judith Howard, "Graphic Representation as Tools for Decision Making," *Social Education*, May 2001

- *Teaching students the many expository text structures that writers use, and showing students how to organize the material graphically, can have a positive effect on comprehension. Demonstrating how to diagram the various expository text structures enables students to "see" how texts are constructed.*

  Susan Dymock, "Teaching Expository Text Structure Awareness," *The Reading Teacher*, October 2005

Contents

Nonfiction Units (continued)

Word Study Units

Introduction

Show Me! Graphic Organizers for Reading Comprehension Across the Curriculum includes thirty-two units that teach, reinforce, and assess a variety of reading comprehension strategies tied to state and national standards. Each unit includes six pages:

1. *Lesson Plan:* includes a description of the strategy and four sections—*Introduce, Model, Practice,* and *Extend and Assess*

2. *Reading Selection:* brief original fiction or nonfiction selection incorporating the strategy

3. *Organizer—Sample:* a completed graphic organizer page based on the reading selection

4. *Organizer—Master:* a graphic organizer blackline master page, including a list of strategy cue words and phrases when applicable

5. *Writing Assignment:* a blackline master for a writing assignment related to the strategy in which the graphic organizer is used as a planning sheet, including sample topic ideas when applicable

6. *Follow-up:* extension activities and a strategy assessment

Show Me! is aimed at classroom teachers, resource teachers, and home-schooling parents of intermediate students. However, it can easily be adapted up or down according to grade or ability level. Here, teachers will find easily accessible instructional materials with which to address required reading comprehension strategies, while students will gain the knowledge and tools they need to apply these strategies in a variety of reading experiences.

How Do I Use Each Component?

Getting Ready

✔ Read the first page of the unit (*Lesson Plan*) to acquaint yourself with the strategy.

✔ Make an overhead transparency of the blank graphic organizer (*Organizer—Master*).

✔ Make three photocopies of the blank graphic organizer for each student in your class (one for reading practice, one for the writing activity, and one for an extension activity).

✔ Make one copy of the writing blackline master (*Writing Assignment*) for each student.

Introducing the Strategy

✔ Conduct the "Introduce the Strategy" activity with the class.

✔ Invite students to discuss their reactions, and answer any questions they pose.

Modeling the Strategy

✔ Place the blank graphic organizer transparency on the overhead. Explain whether you'll use the organizer before, during, and/or after reading and why.

✔ Read the unit's original fiction or nonfiction selection (*Reading Selection*) aloud.

✔ Using the example in the unit (*Organizer— Sample*), model how to fill out the graphic organizer based on the information in the reading selection.

✔ Because filling out a graphic organizer is a prerequisite to note-taking, show students how to utilize key words and phrases when applicable rather than always writing in complete sentences.

✔ Model how to use the completed graphic organizer to summarize the reading selection. (*Note*: Because graphic organizers are summaries, summarizing is included in each unit rather than as a separate strategy.)

✔ Invite students to discuss their reactions, and answer any questions they pose.

Practicing the Strategy

✔ Give each student a blank copy of the graphic organizer.

✔ Make sure students understand whether to use the organizer before, during, and/or after reading and why.

Lesson Plan page

Reading Selection page

Organizer—Sample page

✔ Have students use the blank organizer to practice the strategy in another fiction or nonfiction text, assisting as needed.

✔ Have students use the completed graphic organizers to summarize their reading selections to a partner.

✔ Invite students to discuss their reactions, and answer any questions they pose.

Utilizing the Strategy in Writing

✔ Give each student a blank copy of the graphic organizer and a copy of the writing blackline master.

✔ Have students use the blank organizer as a pre-writing tool to record an example of the strategy from a brief reading selection or a math, science, or social studies lesson. Then have them write a paragraph based on the graphic organizer information.

✔ Have students share their writing with a partner.

✔ Invite students to discuss their reactions, and answer any questions they pose.

Extending the Strategy

✔ Have students complete one or more of the unit's extension activities (*Follow-up*).

Assessing the Strategy

✔ Have students sketch their own graphic organizers on notebook paper (minus the cue lists, if provided).

✔ Select an appropriate reading selection, or write the unit assessment statements on the board. *Note*: Some of the assessments involve reading aloud to the students. If you have access to multiple copies of a suitable text students can read themselves, feel free to use it instead.

✔ Have students analyze the selection or statements, paying special attention to cue words and phrases where applicable, and record the information on their graphic organizers.

✔ Conduct one-on-one or small-group conferences to review students' graphic organizers, clarify any confusion, and answer any questions they still have about the strategy.

✔ Use this information to plan additional instruction, if needed, along with opportunities for periodic review and practice.

Organizer—Master page

Writing Assignment page

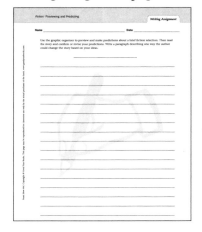

Follow-up page

Additional Tips

- Make sure the reading materials students use when practicing are at their independent reading levels. If learners are struggling with the words, they won't be able to concentrate on the strategy.

- Whenever possible, utilize grade-appropriate magazines for brief fiction and nonfiction reading selections.

- If some students need additional support before practicing the strategy on their own, pair them or pull them aside as a small group to read a selection and fill out a blank graphic organizer as many times as needed.

- If the whole class does not require instruction in a particular strategy, follow the Introduce-Model-Practice-Extend and Assess procedure with individuals, partners, or small groups.

- Make additional copies of the graphic organizers to hang in the classroom. If possible, enlarge them to poster size and laminate. Explain that learning to select an appropriate graphic organizer for a text is a strategy in itself.

- If no overhead projector is available, draw the graphic organizer on the chalkboard or on chart paper when modeling.

- Teach students that graphic organizers are not static. They should feel free to add lines, rows, columns, circles, boxes, and so on to suit their own recording purposes.

- Utilize modeling, demonstrations, and think-alouds at every phase of the strategy acquisition process until students are skilled and confident enough to carry out the steps on their own.

Fiction Units

Previewing and Predicting

How do you select a novel at the library or a bookstore? Likely, the title catches your eye. Next, you look at the cover illustration and read the book jacket blurbs. If you're still interested, you skim the chapter titles. Finally, you read the first paragraph or page. You're hooked! By previewing the book, you get into a certain frame of mind. You know whether the book will be funny, dramatic, scary, or exciting. You also start making predictions about the story. *The man on the cover is the bad guy*, you think to yourself. *The heroine will have to outsmart him . . . their families will get involved . . .* and so on. You can't wait to get home so you can begin reading and confirm or revise your predictions. Previewing and predicting helps readers get the most out of a story by setting the stage, engaging their interest, and focusing their thoughts.

Introduce the Strategy

Think of a true story from your childhood, make up a title for it, and bring a photograph that relates to it in some way. Tell students you're going to share an oral story. Then state the title and show them the photograph. Ask: *What do you predict my story will be about? Why? Who do you predict some of the characters will be? How do you know? What do you predict the mood of the story will be? Why do you think so?* Allow time for discussion. Then explain that looking ahead (previewing) and making good guesses (predicting) helps them get ready to listen to your story. Tell the story and then ask the students to confirm or revise their prediction statements.

Model

Read "I'll Get You for This" on page 8 aloud. Then model how to complete the accompanying graphic organizer (page 9) and use it to summarize the reading selection.

Practice

Have students use a copy of the blank graphic organizer on page 10 to preview and make predictions about other fiction texts, assisting as needed.

Extend and Assess

Have students complete the related writing assignment on page 11 and one or more of the extension activities on page 12. Finally, monitor their acquisition of previewing and predicting by using the page 12 assessment.

Use the Graphic Organizer:

✔ Before Reading
  During Reading
✔ After Reading

I'll Get You for This!

This story reveals the sometimes "rocky" relationship between a boy and his younger brother growing up in Tennessee in the early 1900s.

"Give that back!" Levi hollered, scrambling barefoot between the rows of corn after his brother Tom. "That's my lucky rock!" Levi captured Tom's shirttail just in time to see the treasured stone soar through the air and plummet to the bull's-eye of the bramble patch.

Levi pummeled Tom's back with his fists as Mama scurried out of the cabin. "What's going on here?" she demanded, pulling the boys apart by their overall straps.

"Levi let my toad go," Tom said matter-of-factly, "so I threw his rock in the stickers."

"I'd say you both need to think with your hands for awhile," replied Mama. "Pop is probably on his way, so you can tend to the weeds while I start supper." Levi dropped to his knees between the bushy snap bean plants, and Tom seized the hoe.

"Hi, Pop," shouted Levi to the tall figure striding up the path. "We're weeding the garden." Glancing at Tom, Levi grinned. "After supper I'm going to read to Mama while Tom washes the dishes, cleans our sleep loft, carries water from the spring, and feeds the chickens."

Tom scowled as Pop ruffled his hair. "That's my boys!" Pop declared.

"I'll get you for this, Levi!" Tom said under his breath. "I'll get you. . . ."

Reading Selection Title   <u>I'll Get You for This!</u>

Preview the available text features. Add notes about what you learn from them. Then make two predictions about the story. After reading, mark whether your predictions are confirmed or if you have to revise them.

Text Feature	Notes
title	Someone in the story is upset.
front cover illustration	
story blurb	The boys are brothers. They lived long ago. Sometimes they don't get along.
chapter headings	
chapter illustrations	
first paragraph or page	Tom throws Levi's favorite rock into the stickers.
other	

I predict that this story will be about ___<u>a boy who makes his brother mad</u>___ .

      <u>**X**</u> confirmed   _____ had to revise

I also predict that ___<u>the boys will talk over the problem</u>___ .

     _____ confirmed   <u>**X**</u> had to revise

Now use your graphic organizer to summarize the reading selection to a partner.

Name _____ **Date** _____

Reading Selection Title _____

Preview the available text features. Add notes about what you learn from them. Then make two predictions about the story. After reading, mark whether your predictions are confirmed or if you have to revise them.

Text Feature	Notes
title	
front cover illustration	
story blurb	
chapter headings	
chapter illustrations	
first paragraph or page	
other	

I predict that this story will be about _____ .

_____ confirmed   _____ had to revise

I also predict that _____ .

_____ confirmed   _____ had to revise

Now use your graphic organizer to summarize the reading selection to a partner.

Name _____ **Date** _____

Use the graphic organizer to preview and make predictions about a brief fiction selection. Then read the story and confirm or revise your predictions. Write a paragraph describing one way the author could change the story based on your ideas.

_____

_____

_____

_____

_____

_____

_____

_____

_____

_____

_____

_____

_____

Extension Activities

Have students:

- repeat the "Introduce the Strategy" activity by sharing stories about their own experiences.

- make a list of captivating book titles and explain what they can predict from each one.

- locate library books that have intriguing book-jacket blurbs and share them with the class.

- collect several books and stories with exciting first paragraphs to share with the class.

- write blurbs for their own stories to help readers preview and make predictions.

- add illustrations to their stories to help readers preview and make predictions.

Strategy Assessment

Obtain a selection of short fiction books or magazine stories from the library. Have students sketch their own preview/predict graphic organizers on notebook paper. Then have each student analyze one of the selections and record the results on his or her organizer. After reading, have students confirm or revise their predictions.

Conduct one-on-one or small-group conferences to review students' graphic organizers, clarify any confusion, and answer any questions they still have about the strategy. Use this information to plan additional instruction, if needed, along with opportunities for periodic review and practice.

Asking Questions and Setting a Purpose for Reading

You've read the title, story blurb, chapter headings, and first paragraph or page. You've looked at the cover and chapter illustrations. You've made predictions about the story. However, you also have questions. For example, you might wonder why you see a bird on the cover and why some of the chapter headings include bird names. By asking these questions, you've set a purpose for reading the story. You want to find out how birds fit into the story plot. With this in mind, you're motivated to read and you'll find yourself focusing on the most important information. You may find the answers to your questions right away, or you may not find them until you reach the last word. You'll also ask and answer new questions as you get involved in the story.

Introduce the Strategy

Display an unusual object that most of the students won't have seen before such as an antique, vintage game piece, knick-knack, or tool used by a cook, seamstress, artist, or woodworker. Pair students and have them list questions about the object, such as *What is it? Where did it come from? How old is it? Who uses it?* After you tell about the object and demonstrate its use, if applicable, have the partners revisit their lists and write the answers to their questions. If any questions are unanswered, discuss ways to remedy the situation, such as asking an expert, researching in the library, or using an Internet search engine to locate more information.

Model

Read "Haiku Hannah" on page 14 aloud. Then model how to complete the accompanying graphic organizer (page 15) and use it to summarize the reading selection.

Practice

Have students use a copy of the blank graphic organizer on page 16 to record questions and set a purpose for reading other fiction texts, assisting as needed.

Extend and Assess

Have students complete the related writing assignment on page 17 and one or more of the extension activities on page 18. Finally, monitor their acquisition of questioning and setting a purpose for reading by using the page 18 assessment.

Use the Graphic Organizer:

✔ Before Reading
✔ During Reading
✔ After Reading

Haiku Hannah

"What're you doing, Peter?" asked Hannah.

"I have to think of a haiku poem for homework tonight," Peter grumbled. "A haiku doesn't rhyme, but it has a special syllable pattern—five, then seven, then five again. Writing a haiku is hard!"

"I don't think it's hard. I make haikus all the time. Don't complain to me," said Hannah.

"Hey! That was a haiku!" exclaimed Peter.

"Yes, I know it was. Counting syllables is fun. Just try it, Peter!" Hannah replied.

"That was a haiku, too!" Peter said with a grin.

Hannah put her hands on her hips. "Don't be so surprised. My name is Haiku Hannah. Now what do you say?"

"I get it, Hannah! Thank you for showing me how. This homework's easy!" Peter announced.

Hannah patted Peter's shoulder. "You have a new name. I'll call you Poetry Pete. We make a great pair!"

Reading Selection Title ___Haiku Hannah___

Record questions you have about the story and set a purpose for reading. Then record the answers, if found, and whether or not you accomplished your goal.

Question	Was it answered?	If so, what's the answer?
How did Hannah get her name?	__X__ Yes _____ No	She likes to make haikus.
What is a haiku?	__X__ Yes _____ No	A haiku is an unrhymed poem with a 5-7-5 syllable pattern.
Is it hard to write a haiku?	__X__ Yes _____ No	Peter thinks haikus are difficult, but Hannah shows that they are easy.
Does Peter figure out how to write one?	__X__ Yes _____ No	Yes.
What haiku does he turn in for his homework?	_____ Yes __X__ No	
	_____ Yes _____ No	

I'll read this story to ___find out why the author chose this title___ .

Outcome: ___the title describes a talent of one of the main characters.___

Now use your graphic organizer to summarize the reading selection to a partner.

Name _____ **Date** _____

Reading Selection Title _____

Record questions you have about the story and set a purpose for reading. Then record the answers, if found, and whether or not you accomplished your goal.

Question	Was it answered?	If so, what's the answer?
	_____ Yes _____ No	
	_____ Yes _____ No	
	_____ Yes _____ No	
	_____ Yes _____ No	
	_____ Yes _____ No	
	_____ Yes _____ No	

I'll read this story to _____ .

Outcome: _____

Now use your graphic organizer to summarize the reading selection to a partner.

Name _____ **Date** _____

Use the graphic organizer to ask questions and set a purpose for reading a brief fiction selection. Then read the story and write a paragraph about one of the answers you found.

_____

_____

_____

_____

_____

_____

_____

_____

_____

_____

_____

_____

_____

_____

Extension Activities

Have students:

- repeat the "Introduce the Strategy" activity by bringing in their own unusual objects and answering questions about them.

- use the graphic organizer to ask questions and set a purpose for reading the next chapter in your current classroom read-aloud.

- find newspaper articles with questions in the titles and highlight the answers in the text.

- locate library books in which the book-jacket blurbs state a purpose for reading.

- use the graphic organizer to ask questions and set a purpose for watching a favorite weekly sitcom at home and then share their results with the class.

- write a new ending to a story that answers a previously unanswered question.

Strategy Assessment

Have students sketch their own questions/purpose graphic organizers on notebook paper. Locate a brief, interesting story from a grade-appropriate magazine or anthology. Read the title aloud. If the title doesn't indicate what the story is about, provide a one-sentence summary. Allow time for students to fill in the before-reading sections of the graphic organizer. Then read the story aloud and have students complete their organizers.

Conduct one-on-one or small-group conferences to review students' graphic organizers, clarify any confusion, and answer any questions they still have about the strategy. Use this information to plan additional instruction, if needed, along with opportunities for periodic review and practice.

Analyzing Story Elements

When you read a story, you become a detective. First you scrutinize the setting: *Where does the story take place? When does the story occur?* Then you investigate the characters: *Who is the story about? What are they like?* Finally, you explore the plot: *What happens in the story? Why does it happen? What are the characters' goals? What actions do they take to attain their goals? How are the story problems solved? What is the final outcome?* By analyzing story elements, readers enjoy stories more, understand them better, and remember them longer.

Introduce the Strategy

Divide the class into groups of three and give each student a slip of paper. Student #1 secretly lists two characters and a brief description of each, such as: *Chloe, a fifth-grade girl who loves soccer, and Logan, her older brother who plays drums in a band.* Student #2 secretly lists a setting, including time and place, such as: *a summer evening in the courtyard of a city apartment complex.* Student #3 secretly lists a problem, such as: *someone borrows a special item from a friend and accidentally loses it.* Finally, have the students in each group put their elements together and use them to create an oral or written story. Tell them they can add additional characters, settings, and events, but the problem should be solved by the end of the story.

Model

Read "Calf Boy Helps His Father" on page 20 aloud. Then model how to complete the accompanying graphic organizer (page 21) and use it to summarize the reading selection.

Practice

Have students use a copy of the blank graphic organizer on page 22 to analyze story elements in other fiction texts, assisting as needed.

Extend and Assess

Have students complete the related writing assignment on page 23 and one or more of the extension activities on page 24. Finally, monitor their acquisition of story element analysis by using the page 24 assessment.

Use the Graphic Organizer:

Before Reading

✔ During Reading

✔ After Reading

Calf Boy Helps His Father (Retold)

Calf Boy and his parents lived with his father's family, who did not like Calf Boy's mother, Buffalo Woman. One day when Calf Boy's father was out hunting, the family told Buffalo Woman and Calf Boy to leave. "You are not like us. Go live with the animals where you belong," they said.

Calf Boy knew his father would come for them, so he made sure to leave footprints along the trail. When they stopped to camp, Buffalo Woman made enough supper for herself, Calf Boy, and her husband. Sure enough, Calf Boy's father soon appeared.

"Your family will never accept me," Buffalo Woman said as they ate together. "I must return to my own nation. They will be happy to see me and will love Calf Boy as their own. But you will be in danger if you follow me there. Goodbye, my love."

Calf Boy knew his father was not afraid. Again he left footprints along the trail. When they reached the buffalo herd,

his father was close behind. An old bull spotted Calf Boy's father and charged at him. "Look out!" shouted Calf Boy.

Calf Boy's father stood his ground. "I have come to be with my wife and child," he said.

"If you can find them in the herd, you may stay," agreed the bull.

"I'll be the calf with the twitching ear," Calf Boy whispered to his father. "Mother will be the cow with the burr on her back." The bull herded Calf Boy and his mother to the far end of the pasture.

Calf Boy's father found his wife and child using the clues. The old bull kept his word and granted the man's wish. The herd circled the man, rolled him in dirt, and gave him a buffalo hide. After three days, Calf Boy's father was a buffalo like the rest. And that is how the buffalo and humans became family and will be until the end of time.

Reading Selection Title ___Calf Boy Helps His Father___

To analyze setting, characters, and plot, answer the following questions as you read the story.

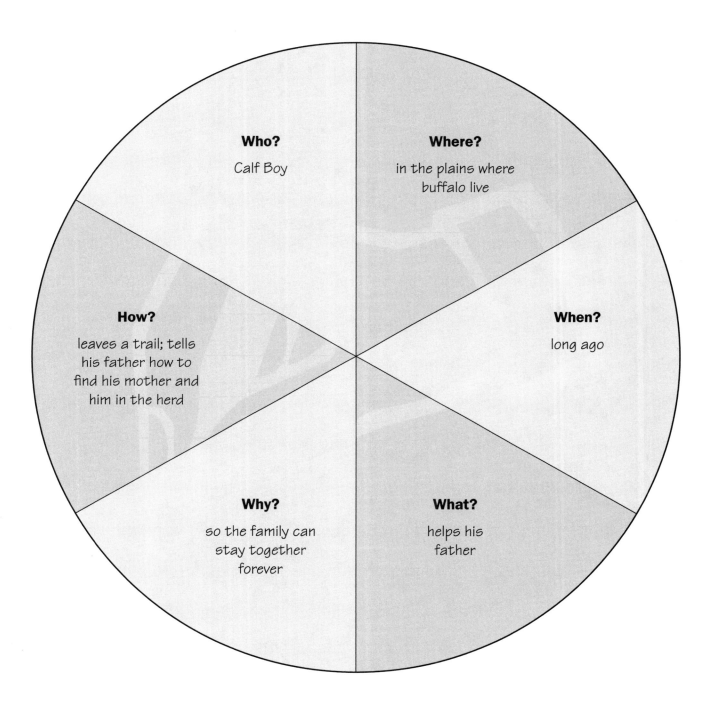

Who?
Calf Boy

Where?
in the plains where
buffalo live

When?
long ago

What?
helps his
father

Why?
so the family can
stay together
forever

How?
leaves a trail; tells
his father how to
find his mother and
him in the herd

Now use your graphic organizer to summarize the reading selection to a partner.

Name _____ **Date** _____

Reading Selection Title _____

To analyze setting, characters, and plot, answer the following questions as you read the story.

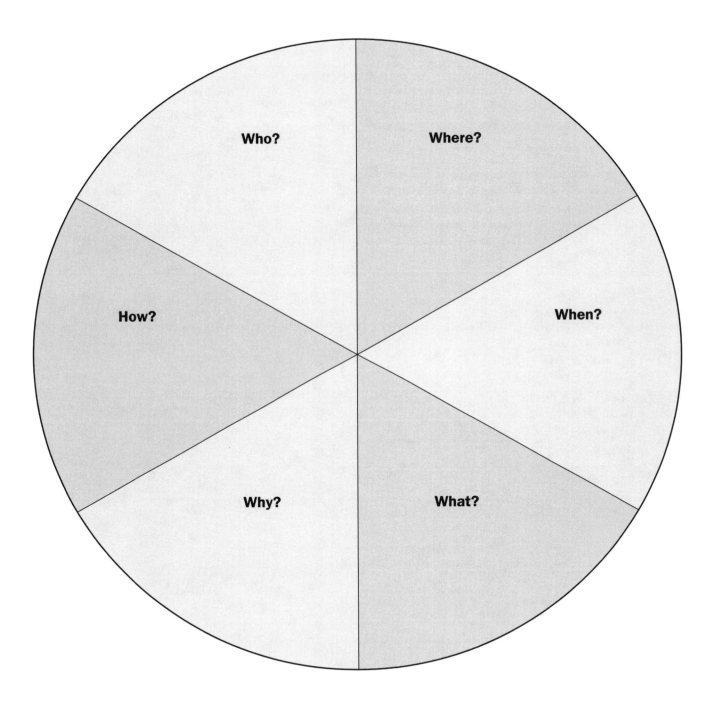

Now use your graphic organizer to summarize the reading selection to a partner.

Name _____ **Date** _____

Read a brief fiction selection and use the graphic organizer to analyze *who, where, when, what, why,* and *how.* Then write a paragraph describing one of the story elements in detail.

_____

_____

_____

_____

_____

_____

_____

_____

_____

_____

_____

_____

_____

_____

_____

_____

_____

Extension Activities

Have students:

- collect photographs of people and places from newspapers and magazines and use them for characters and settings in original stories.

- locate a newspaper article that tells a real-life story and highlight the characters, setting, problem, and solution.

- use the graphic organizer to analyze story elements in your current classroom read-aloud.

- locate library books in which the book-jacket blurbs list the characters, setting, and story problem.

- use the graphic organizer to analyze story elements while watching a movie at home and then share their results with the class.

- write reviews of their favorite fiction books that tell "just enough" about the story elements but don't give away the endings.

Strategy Assessment

Have students sketch their own story elements graphic organizers on notebook paper. Locate a brief, interesting story from a grade-appropriate magazine or anthology. Read it aloud slowly, pausing periodically so students can record information on their graphic organizers. If needed, read it once more at a quicker pace so students can check their work.

Conduct one-on-one or small-group conferences to review students' graphic organizers, clarify any confusion, and answer any questions they still have about the strategy. Use this information to plan additional instruction, if needed, along with opportunities for periodic review and practice.

Making Inferences

Authors know they can't tell every detail in a story. They also know that readers are smart and able to think for themselves. Because authors don't always provide explicit information, good readers draw upon their own knowledge and experiences, combine them with text clues, and use the result to make inferences. Inferring allows us to fill in the gaps, create a mental picture of what is happening, and make logical guesses about the characters, setting, and plot. This, in turn, helps us better understand, enjoy, and remember the stories we read.

Introduce the Strategy

On slips of paper, record situations that can be pantomimed. Have students take turns selecting one and acting out the scenario without speaking while the audience tries to figure out what is happening. For example, a student whose situation is *Everyone in the class got a high score on a test* might smile and nod at his or her classmates and pat them on the back or shake their hands. Point out that audience members need to use the actors' clues along with their own experiences to infer what situation is being pantomimed. Follow up each demonstration by asking: *How do you know?* or *Why do you think that?*

Model

Read "Surprise Visitor" on page 26 aloud. Then model how to complete the accompanying graphic organizer (page 27) and use it to summarize the reading selection.

Practice

Have students use a copy of the blank graphic organizer on page 28 to make inferences in other fiction texts, assisting as needed.

Extend and Assess

Have students complete the related writing assignment on page 29 and one or more of the extension activities on page 30. Finally, monitor their acquisition of inferencing by using the page 30 assessment.

Use the Graphic Organizer:

Before Reading

✔ During Reading

✔ After Reading

Surprise Visitor

"May I have a bedtime snack?" asked Bryan as he stuffed the last of his homework into his backpack on the kitchen table.

"Sure! How about a bowl of cereal? You can fix me one, too," called Mom from the study. "I'll be working late on my presentation. Oh, and don't forget to fill Fluffy's food bowl by the back door, too."

Bryan left briefly and then returned to the kitchen to pour two bowls of cereal, unaware that he was being watched from the next room by the resident mouse. *Spill some! Spill some!* willed the mouse. As if on cue, several cereal flakes fell to the floor. *Now leave!* thought the mouse. The next thing she knew, the human walked out of the kitchen with a bowl in each hand, stopping only to turn off the light.

The mouse waited a few minutes and then peeked around the corner, checking to see if the coast was clear. *Good! The humans are nowhere near*, she said to herself. She looked across the floor and sniffed the air. The cereal's aroma tantalized her nostrils.

The mouse glanced around once more and then crept out from the doorway, continuing to assess her surroundings. Satisfied, she quickened her pace and scurried toward the treat. Then she heard a noise. She stopped in her tracks. She looked around, but saw nothing. *I'm just imagining things*, she reassured herself. She hurried on, her mouth watering for the cereal.

Just as she reached the spilled treasure, she heard the noise again. She spun around, and . . . *YIKES!*

Fiction: Making Inferences

Reading Selection Title   _Surprise Visitor_

Record story clues and use them to make inferences about the setting, characters, or plot.

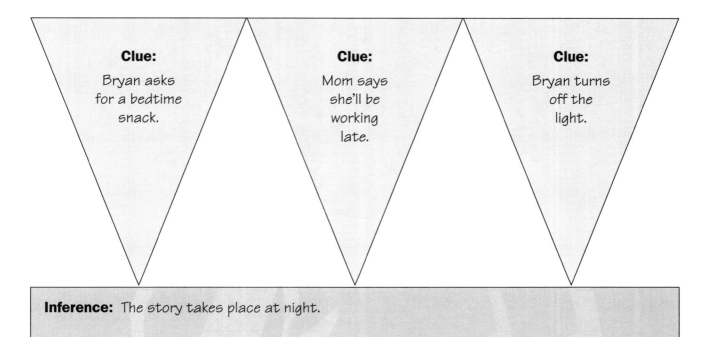

Clue: Bryan asks for a bedtime snack.

Clue: Mom says she'll be working late.

Clue: Bryan turns off the light.

Inference: The story takes place at night.

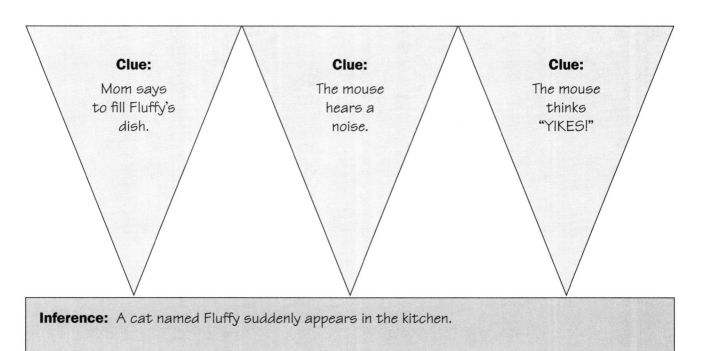

Clue: Mom says to fill Fluffy's dish.

Clue: The mouse hears a noise.

Clue: The mouse thinks "YIKES!"

Inference: A cat named Fluffy suddenly appears in the kitchen.

Now use your graphic organizer to summarize the reading selection to a partner.

Name _____ **Date** _____

Reading Selection Title _____

Record story clues and use them to make inferences about the setting, characters, or plot.

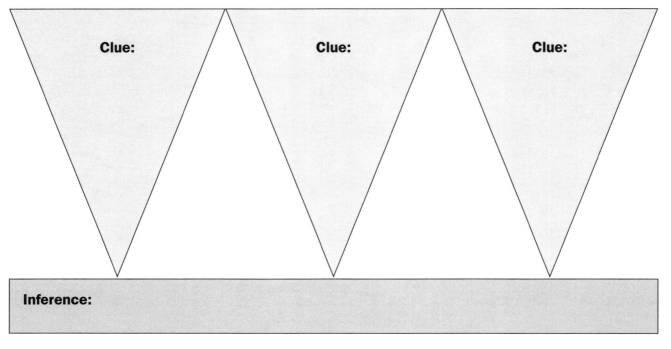

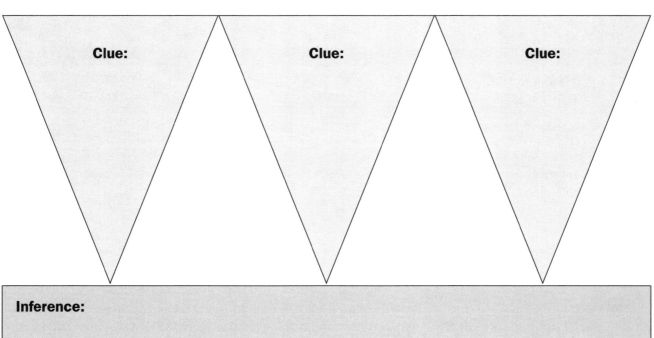

Now use your graphic organizer to summarize the reading selection to a partner.

Name _____ **Date** _____

As you read a brief fiction selection, use the graphic organizer to make inferences. Then write a paragraph about what else could have happened to the main character based on what you inferred.

_____

_____

_____

_____

_____

_____

_____

_____

_____

_____

_____

_____

_____

_____

_____

Extension Activities

Have students:

- use the graphic organizer to record other text clues and inferences they could make from the reading selection on page 26.

- cut out interesting photos from old newspapers or magazines and use the visual clues to create inferences about the photographer.

- share inferences they make from information in their content-area textbooks.

- share examples of times when they or others have made real-life inferences that turned out to be incorrect.

- use the graphic organizer to record clues and inferences in your current classroom read-aloud.

- use the graphic organizer to record clues and inferences while watching a movie at home and then share the results with the class.

Strategy Assessment

Have students sketch their own inference graphic organizers on notebook paper. Locate a brief, interesting story from a grade-appropriate magazine or anthology. Read it aloud slowly, pausing periodically so students can record information on their graphic organizers. If needed, read it once more at a quicker pace so students can check their work.

Conduct one-on-one or small-group conferences to review students' graphic organizers, clarify any confusion, and answer any questions they still have about the strategy. Use this information to plan additional instruction, if needed, along with opportunities for periodic review and practice.

Analyzing Cause and Effect

A cause-and-effect relationship helps explain how or why something happens in a story. Sometimes the narrative or dialogue includes cue words and phrases that indicate cause and effect, such as *due to, because, if/then, as a result,* or *consequently*. Other times the cause and effect aren't directly stated. In this case, the reader must look more closely to discover character actions and plot situations that make (cause) other events (effects) occur. This, in turn, helps the reader better understand the characters, their decisions and relationships, and why they do the things they do.

Introduce the Strategy

Locate an interesting photo in a newspaper or magazine. As you display it for the class, think aloud about what might happen next. For example, if the photo shows a choir singing, say: *After the choir finishes singing this song, the audience will probably clap for them*. Then identify the cause and the effect in the relationship: *The choir performance* causes *the audience to clap. Clapping is the effect.* Next, have students locate their own photos to share with the class. Ask: *What might happen next?* As students answer, have the class identify the cause and effect.

Model

Read "No One But Me" on page 32 aloud. Then model how to complete the accompanying graphic organizer (page 33) and use it to summarize the reading selection.

Practice

Have students use a copy of the blank graphic organizer on page 34 to analyze cause and effect in other fiction texts, assisting as needed.

Extend and Assess

Have students complete the related writing assignment on page 35 and one or more of the extension activities on page 36. Finally, monitor their acquisition of cause-and-effect analysis by using the page 36 assessment.

Use the Graphic Organizer:

Before Reading

✔ During Reading

✔ After Reading

No One But Me

My buddies and I jumped when my big sister burst through the kitchen door. "Hey, Jenna," I said. "We're having a snack before we play some basketball. Do you want a cookie?" Jenna looked around the room, stopping to stare into our eyes one by one. No one moved. Suddenly, she pointed at Tony. "You!" she said through clenched teeth. "We need to have a talk!"

We froze in our seats as Tony slowly rose from his chair. His eyes were wide and his hands trembled. No one seemed to know what was happening. No one but me, that is.

As the door closed, Juan looked at me, frowning. "Why is your sister so upset, Lucas?" he asked.

I shrugged, and everyone kept eating. Although it seemed like hours, Tony returned a couple of minutes later with his pet mouse, Rascal, peeking out of his pocket. Jenna followed close behind. I tried not to make eye contact, but I guess that was a dead giveaway. Soon I was the next victim of Jenna's pointing finger.

When I returned to the kitchen, everyone was already in the yard. They all crowded around me as I joined them, bouncing my basketball. "What happened?" they demanded.

"I have to do my sister's chores for the next two weeks," I said with a sigh.

"What did you do?" asked Tony. "All Jenna asked me was where I left Rascal when I came over."

"Well, tomorrow's April Fool's Day and Jenna will be gone to a debate tournament, so I decided to trick her early," I said. "I thought she'd find it amusing to reach into her bookbag for her computer mouse and find Rascal instead. But I was wrong."

All the guys fell onto the grass, laughing. "I guess the trick's on you, Lucas!" said Tony.

Reading Selection Title _____No One But Me_____

Mark the following cue words you find in the reading selection. Then record causes and effects.

X because	___ subsequently	___ as a result	___ resulting from
___ so	___ due to	X when	___ effect
___ since	___ consequently	___ caused	___ in order to
___ therefore	___ if / then	___ which led to	___ unless

Cause	Effect
Because . . . the door opened unexpectedly,	the boys jumped.
Because . . . the boys were trying to figure out what Jenna wanted,	no one moved.
Because . . . Jenna's teeth were clenched,	the boys knew she was upset.
Because . . . the boys were worried about Tony,	time seemed to go by slowly.
Because . . . Lucas didn't make eye contact with Jenna,	she knew he was guilty.
Because . . . Tony owned Rascal,	Jenna thought he had put the mouse in her backpack.
Because . . . Lucas was the one who really put Rascal in the backpack,	he had to do Jenna's chores for the next two weeks.
Because . . .	

Now use your graphic organizer to summarize the reading selection to a partner.

Name _____ **Date** _____

Reading Selection Title _____

Mark the following cue words you find in the reading selection. Then record causes and effects.

___ because	___ subsequently	___ as a result	___ resulting from
___ so	___ due to	___ when	___ effect
___ since	___ consequently	___ caused	___ in order to
___ therefore	___ if / then	___ which led to	___ unless

Cause	Effect
Because . . .	
Because . . .	
Because . . .	
Because . . .	
Because . . .	
Because . . .	
Because . . .	
Because . . .	

Now use your graphic organizer to summarize the reading selection to a partner.

Name _____ **Date** _____

As you read a brief fiction selection, use the graphic organizer to analyze cause-and-effect relationships. Then write a paragraph about another effect that could have occurred in the story.

_____

_____

_____

_____

_____

_____

_____

_____

_____

_____

_____

_____

_____

_____

_____

_____

Extension Activities

Have students:

- repeat the Introduce the Strategy activity using different photographs.

- write a sequel to "No One But Me" and include some cause-and-effect relationships that occur as Lucas does his sister's chores for two weeks.

- cut out newspaper or magazine articles about real-life events and highlight the cause-and-effect cue words and phrases.

- draw an example of a cause and effect, trade with a classmate, and add captions or speech balloons to each other's drawings.

- share a humorous, real-life incident in which one event caused a chain reaction of other events.

- use the graphic organizer to record cause and effects in a movie watched at home and then share the results with the class.

Strategy Assessment

Have students sketch their own cause-and-effect graphic organizers on notebook paper (minus the cue list). Locate a brief, interesting story from a grade-appropriate magazine or anthology. Read it aloud slowly, pausing periodically so students can record information on their graphic organizers. Remind them to listen for cue words and phrases as well. If needed, read it once more at a quicker pace so students can check their work.

Conduct one-on-one or small-group conferences to review students' graphic organizers, clarify any confusion, and answer any questions they still have about the strategy. Use this information to plan additional instruction, if needed, along with opportunities for periodic review and practice.

Comparing and Contrasting Characters

Because story characters are the heart and soul of fiction, we pay close attention to their physical characteristics, personality traits, goals, and actions. We get even more out of the story if we take time to compare and contrast the characters. Comparing means looking for ways the characters are similar. Contrasting means looking for ways they are different. Sometimes the author uses compare/contrast cue words in the narrative or dialogue, such as *like, also, however, or but.* However, it's usually up to the reader to make these connections.

Introduce the Strategy

Write character names from well-known books, TV shows, and movies on slips of paper. Have students take turns selecting one and stating three words or phrases that describe that character as you record their ideas on the board. After everyone has had a turn, analyze the results together. Ask: *Do any of the characters have traits in common? What are some ways they are different from each other?* Explain that this process is called comparing and contrasting and is a useful tool for thinking about the roles of characters in stories.

Model

Read "What in the World Is a Farthingale?" on page 38 aloud. Then model how to complete the accompanying graphic organizer (page 39) and use it to summarize the reading selection.

Practice

Have students use a copy of the blank graphic organizer on page 40 to compare and contrast characters in other fiction texts, assisting as needed.

Extend and Assess

Have students complete the related writing assignment on page 41 and one or more of the extension activities on page 42. Finally, monitor their acquisition of character comparisons and contrasts by using the page 42 assessment.

Use the Graphic Organizer:

Before Reading
✔ During Reading
✔ After Reading

What in the World Is a Farthingale?

"Today we'll start with a partner activity," said Mrs. Rathburn. "I want you to list all the outerwear clothing items you can think of. You'll get a point for each word no one else in the class uses. Your partner assignments are on these slips of paper."

Gracie! Luis said to himself, running his fingers through his cropped dark hair. *Oh, great! I hardly know her.* Gracie bounced over to Luis's desk, pulled up a chair, and leaned on her elbows. "Hi!" she said, grinning. "I notice we have something in common—we're wearing the same brand of sneakers. Go figure! Do you like my fingernails? I painted them purple last night. Well, enough about me. I'm gabby but you're shy, so I'll talk and you write. We're both going to get LOTS of points."

"Okay," Luis mumbled. He opened his notebook, grabbed a pencil, and started writing. *Shirt . . . pants . . . jeans . . . socks . . . gloves. . . .*

"That's a great start, but now try these," said Gracie. "*Doublet, cloak, kilt, toga, tunic, breeches, farthingale. . . .*"

"Whoa!" said Luis, putting down his pencil and flexing his fingers. "Slow down! And what in the world is a farthingale?"

"It's one of those big hoop skirts women used to wear," said Gracie. "You read all the time—haven't you ever tried historical fiction?"

"No, I read science fiction instead," said Luis. "But these are cool words."

"I'll show you some good old-time books if you want to meet me in the library after school," said Gracie. "I especially like the ones about swashbucklers."

"Whatever those are, I'll probably like them too," said Luis. "I'll be there! Now— my hand's rested, so let's get busy and win this contest!"

Reading Selection Title ___What in the World Is a Farthingale?___

Mark the following cue words or phrases you find in the reading selection. Then record things that are different and things that are alike about two characters.

X too	___ like	___ however	___ unless	___ otherwise
X both	___ also	X but	___ while	___ either
___ alike	___ similar	___ yet	___ different	___ on the contrary
___ likewise	___ in addition	___ on the other hand	___ unlike	___ even though
X same	___ as well as	___ although	___ in contrast	X instead
___ all	X in common	___ more/less	___ not only	

Character #1: Luis	**Both Characters**	**Character #2:** Gracie
Physical characteristics: cropped dark hair	**Physical characteristics:** wear the same brand of sneakers	**Physical characteristics:** purple fingernails
Personality traits: quiet shy likes science fiction	**Personality traits:** compliment/encourage one another like to read	**Personality traits:** outgoing "gabby" likes historical fiction
Goals: wants to learn some new "cool" words	**Goals:** want to win the contest	**Goals:** wants to share her love of "old-time" books
Actions: agrees to meet Gracie at the library after school	**Actions:** keep adding words to the list	**Actions:** offers to show Luis some books after school

Now use your graphic organizer to summarize the reading selection to a partner.

Name _____ Date _____

Reading Selection Title _____

Mark the following cue words or phrases you find in the reading selection. Then record things that are different and things that are alike about two characters.

___ too	___ like	___ however	___ unless	___ otherwise
___ both	___ also	___ but	___ while	___ either
___ alike	___ similar	___ yet	___ different	___ on the contrary
___ likewise	___ in addition	___ on the other hand	___ unlike	___ even though
___ same	___ as well as	___ although	___ in contrast	___ instead
___ all	___ in common	___ more/less	___ not only	

Character #1:	Both Characters	Character #2:
Physical characteristics:	**Physical characteristics:**	**Physical characteristics:**
Personality traits:	**Personality traits:**	**Personality traits:**
Goals:	**Goals:**	**Goals:**
Actions:	**Actions:**	**Actions:**

Now use your graphic organizer to summarize the reading selection to a partner.

Name _____   **Date** _____

Use the graphic organizer to compare and contrast characters in a short fiction selection. Then write a paragraph about a situation your favorite character might experience in another story and why.

_____

_____

_____

_____

_____

_____

_____

_____

_____

_____

_____

_____

_____

_____

Extension Activities

Have students:

- write their own stories about working with a partner and then compare and contrast the characters.

- take turns making *I'm like* _____ *because* . . . statements about characters they've encountered in classroom read-alouds.

- make a list of traits, such as *strong, kind, brave, mean, creative,* and *funny*, and think of one or more story characters each word describes.

- make labeled drawings of two story characters noting ways they are different and alike.

- use the graphic organizer to compare and contrast two people mentioned in a news article about an interesting incident or event.

- use the graphic organizer to make inferences about ways two people in a painting or photograph are different and alike.

Strategy Assessment

Have students sketch their own character compare/contrast graphic organizers on notebook paper (minus the cue list). Locate a brief, interesting story from a grade-appropriate magazine or anthology that includes at least two strong characters. Read it aloud slowly, pausing periodically so students can record information on their graphic organizers. Remind them to listen for cue words and phrases as well. If needed, read it once more at a quicker pace so students can check their work.

Conduct one-on-one or small-group conferences to review students' graphic organizers, clarify any confusion, and answer any questions they still have about the strategy. Use this information to plan additional instruction, if needed, along with opportunities for periodic review and practice.

Retelling to Monitor Meaning

Almost everyone loves to tell stories they have read, heard, or experienced. Retelling benefits the audience, who gets to enjoy the tale, but it also benefits the storyteller, who works hard to remember and process the important details, organize them, and present them in a meaningful order. The most common structure for retelling is *beginning, middle,* and *end.* In the beginning, the reteller describes the characters and setting. In the middle, the reteller describes the story problem, and in the end, he or she retells how the problem is solved. In this way, retellers not only check their understanding of the story as a whole but make sure all the important elements are included. Retelling is the vehicle of choice for legends, fables, tall tales, fairy tales, and folktales around the world, such as the traditional story "The Goat and the Rock" found in this unit. However, the strategy is equally effective for contemporary fiction, historical fiction, science fiction, and other imaginative genres.

Introduce the Strategy

Locate a short story that no one in the class has read. Read aloud the first sentence, one from the middle, and the last sentence. Then have the students work with partners or in small groups to concoct an oral story to match this sketchy outline. After everyone has had a chance to share their stories with the class, read the original aloud and discuss the similarities and differences in the various versions presented. Point out that the beginning, middle, and end of the story are important, but in-between details are vital as well.

Model

Read "The Goat and the Rock" on page 44 aloud. Then model how to complete the accompanying graphic organizer (page 45) and use it to summarize the reading selection.

Practice

Have students use a copy of the blank graphic organizer on page 46 to retell other fiction texts, assisting as needed.

Extend and Assess

Have students complete the related writing assignment on page 47 and one or more of the extension activities on page 48. Finally, monitor their acquisition of retelling by using the page 48 assessment.

Use the Graphic Organizer:

Before Reading

✔ During Reading

After Reading

The Goat and the Rock (Retold)

Long ago in Tibet, a boy carried a jug about the village. "Milk for sale!" he called. "Get your fresh milk here!" Thirsty people brought their cups for him to fill, paid him, and went on their way.

One day the boy was tired, so he set his jug on a large, flat rock and stretched out on a grassy hill to rest. Soon a girl came along with her herd of goats. One of them accidentally knocked over the jug, breaking it to pieces. The boy jumped up. "Your goat broke my jug!" he shouted. "You must pay for it!"

"Oh, no," replied the girl. "The rock broke your jug."

Your goat! The rock! Your goat! The rock! The two went back and forth until a growing group of onlookers called for the village ruler. "I'll settle this fight," he said to the boy and girl. "The goat and the rock must come with me. A jury will figure out who's to blame." Then he ordered the goat and the rock brought to the court.

People ran from far and near. "Come one! Come all!" they called. "The village ruler has lost his mind! He's trying a goat and a rock!"

Soon the courtroom was full and people were lined up outside as far as the eye could see. The ruler smiled and addressed the crowd. "I've tricked you all. Each of you must pay a fine for thinking so little of me. The goat and the rock may go."

The people laughed at their own foolishness and handed over the money. Several strong men carried the rock back to the hill. The wise ruler gave the boy enough coins to buy a new jug. The grateful girl let the boy milk her goat and then went happily on her way.

"Milk for sale!" called the boy, as he walked about the village. "Get your fresh milk here!"

Reading Selection Title   The Goat and the Rock

Record the most important story events in the order they happen.

Title: The Goat and the Rock

Beginning: A boy sells milk around the village.

He's tired and stops for a rest, setting his milk jug on a rock.

Middle: A girl's goat accidentally knocks over the jug and breaks it.

The boy and girl argue about whether the broken jug is the goat's fault or the rock's fault.

The village ruler declares a trial for the goat and the rock. Everyone comes to watch the spectacle.

End: The ruler charges the onlookers a fine for thinking him a fool.

The ruler lets the goat and the rock go and gives the boy enough money to buy a new jug.

Now use your graphic organizer to summarize the reading selection to a partner.

45

Name _____ **Date** _____

Reading Selection Title _____

Record the most important story events in the order they happen.

Title:

Beginning:

Middle:

End:

Now use your graphic organizer to summarize the reading selection to a partner.

Name _____ **Date** _____

Use the graphic organizer to retell events in a brief fiction selection. Then write your favorite part of the story in your own words.

_____

_____

_____

_____

_____

_____

_____

_____

_____

_____

_____

_____

_____

_____

Extension Activities

Have students:

- practice retelling "The Goat and the Rock" in their own words and then "perform" it for their families or another class.

- retell a story with a series of wordless drawings or cartoons with speech balloons.

- retell a story with a pantomime or skit.

- use the graphic organizer to retell a movie watched at home and then share it with the class.

- use the graphic organizer to retell an epic or a ballad you read aloud to the class.

- retell stories but leave off the endings to entice classmates to read the books on their own.

Strategy Assessment

Have students sketch their own retelling graphic organizers on notebook paper. Locate a brief, interesting story from a grade-appropriate magazine or anthology. Read it aloud slowly, pausing periodically so students can record information on their graphic organizers. If needed, read it once more at a quicker pace so students can check their work.

Conduct one-on-one or small-group conferences to review students' graphic organizers, clarify any confusion, and answer any questions they still have about the strategy. Use this information to plan additional instruction, if needed, along with opportunities for periodic review and practice.

Identifying Story Theme

The theme of a story is the message, lesson, or point the author hopes to convey. In order to provide the *ah-ha!* moment readers seek, the theme should be important and meaningful in some way—even in a humorous story. Figuring out the theme helps readers understand the relationships between the story elements as well as how the author thinks and feels. It also helps them remember the story and apply its message to other texts—and even to their own lives. Fables frequently spell out the theme with a *moral of the story* tagline. However, most authors trust their readers to discern a story's significance, so they simply provide clues along the way.

Introduce the Strategy

List the title of a familiar tale on the board, such as "Little Red Riding Hood." Say: *When I think about things the characters in this story say and do, I try to figure out the point the author is trying to make. Some people might think it's* Never talk to strangers, *while others might think it's* Good always overcomes evil. *Both answers are logical because they're based on what happens to the story characters*. Have students brainstorm the titles of other well-known stories as you list them on the board. Then have them work with partners or in small groups to discuss the "messages" the authors are trying to send.

Model

Read "Because You Can" on page 50 aloud. Then model how to complete the accompanying graphic organizer (page 51) and use it to summarize the reading selection.

Practice

Have students use a copy of the blank graphic organizer on page 52 to identify story themes in other fiction texts, assisting as needed.

Extend and Assess

Have students complete the related writing assignment on page 53 and one or more of the extension activities on page 54. Finally, monitor their acquisition of story theme identification by using the page 54 assessment.

Use the Graphic Organizer:

Before Reading

✔ During Reading

✔ After Reading

Because You Can

"What's the matter, Antonio?" asked Hailey.

"I'm tired of being this age," Antonio replied. "I can't do anything but go to school, do my chores, and hang out with my friends. I want to do something important. At least you're old enough to drive and get a job."

Hailey laughed. "My friends and I were just talking about how easy life was when we were your age. But while we're on the topic of doing something important, come look at this report I'm writing for my senior English class."

"I don't want to read a boring old report," replied Antonio, yawning.

"It's not boring at all," Hailey said. "I researched people who accomplished amazing things at amazingly young ages."

"Do you mean like Anne Frank, who wrote *The Diary of a Young Girl* when she was a teenager?" asked Antonio. "We're reading that in class."

"Yes, she's in my report," said Hailey. "So is Jason Gaes, an eight-year-old boy who wrote a book about cancer. Six-year-old Suzanna Goodin won a national invention contest with an edible spoon-shaped cracker for dipping cat food out of a can. Wolfgang Mozart began composing music before he was five. And an eleven-year-old, Grace Bedell, convinced Abraham Lincoln that he should grow a beard."

"Cool!" said Antonio. "I'm not in the mood to write a book or a symphony or a letter to the president, but I DO have ideas for some great inventions."

"Go for it!" said Hailey. "But don't do it to get into someone's school report someday. Do it for fun . . . and because you can."

Reading Selection Title ___Because You Can___

Record clues that help you determine the theme of the story.

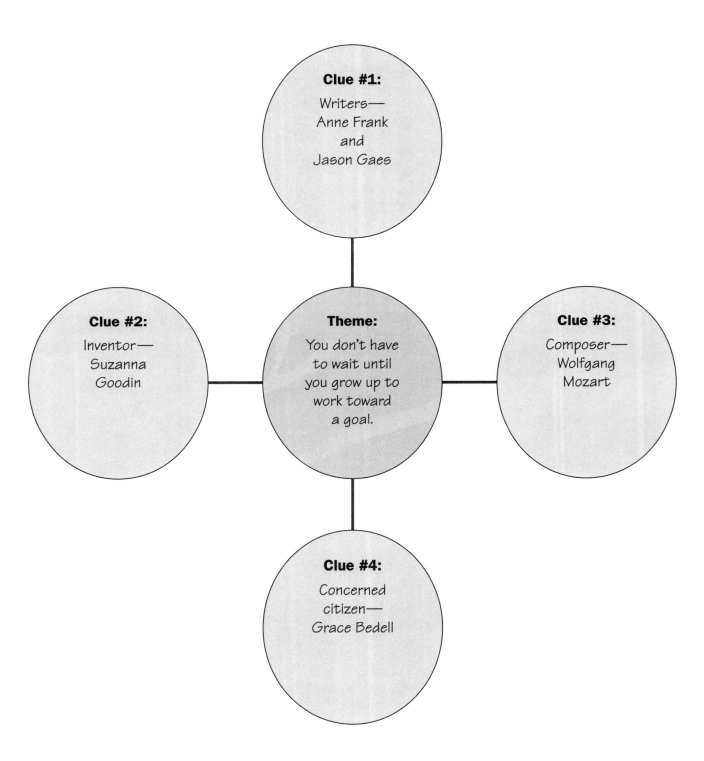

Clue #1:

Writers—
Anne Frank
and
Jason Gaes

Clue #2:

Inventor—
Suzanna
Goodin

Theme:

You don't have
to wait until
you grow up to
work toward
a goal.

Clue #3:

Composer—
Wolfgang
Mozart

Clue #4:

Concerned
citizen—
Grace Bedell

Now use your graphic organizer to summarize the reading selection to a partner.

Name _____ **Date** _____

Reading Selection Title _____

Record clues that help you determine the theme of the story.

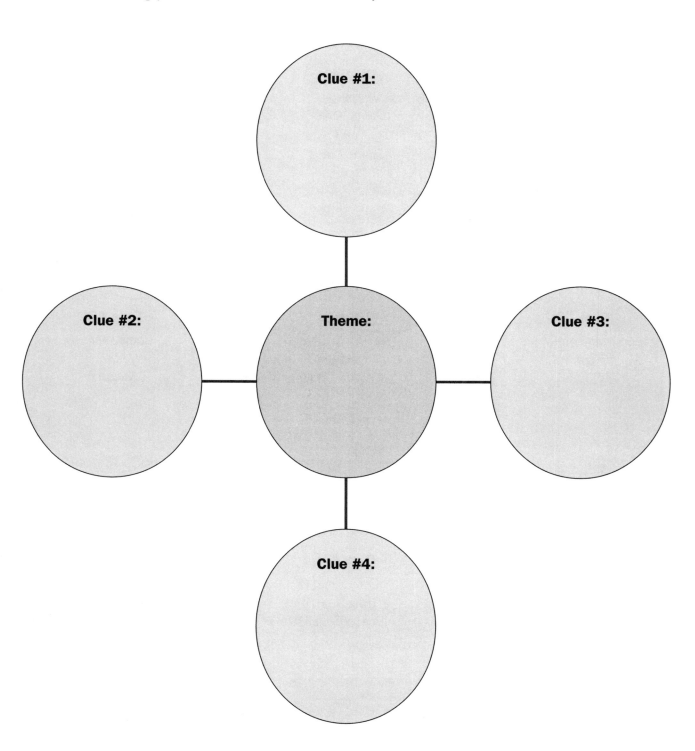

Now use your graphic organizer to summarize the reading selection to a partner.

From *Show Me!*, Copyright © Good Year Books. This page may be reproduced for classroom use only by the actual purchaser of the book. www.goodyearbooks.com

Name _____ **Date** _____

Use the graphic organizer to identify the theme of a brief fiction selection. Then write a paragraph about what the theme means to you.

_____

_____

_____

_____

_____

_____

_____

_____

_____

_____

_____

_____

_____

_____

Extension Activities

Have students:

- write a sequel to "Because You Can" based on Antonio's new insights about working toward goals.

- ask themselves what they learned after reading a particular fiction selection, such as how to make a friend, conquer a fear, or overcome a challenge.

- select stories from their own writing portfolios and try to determine the themes.

- make posters that depict the themes of stories they read.

- use the graphic organizer to determine the theme of a movie they watch at home and then share it with the class.

- use the graphic organizer to determine the theme of a famous art reproduction.

Strategy Assessment

Have students sketch their own story theme graphic organizers on notebook paper. Locate a brief, interesting story from a grade-appropriate magazine or anthology. Read it aloud slowly, pausing periodically so students can record information on their graphic organizers. If needed, read it once more at a quicker pace so students can check their work.

Conduct one-on-one or small-group conferences to review students' graphic organizers, clarify any confusion, and answer any questions they still have about the strategy. Use this information to plan additional instruction, if needed, along with opportunities for periodic review and practice.

Evaluating Stories

Almost everyone who has ever gone to school has given a book report. However, reporting on a book is not always the same as evaluating the story. Evaluation involves assessing how successfully the author sets a scene, makes a character come alive, or develops a plot. It also involves forming opinions and asking yourself questions: *What do I like and dislike about the story? What did I learn? What surprised me? What do I wish the author could clarify? How do I feel about the ending? How does the story relate to my own life? To whom will I recommend the story?* By putting your thoughts and feelings into words, you get more out of the story and store up valuable literacy information that you can apply to new reading and writing situations.

Introduce the Strategy

On a sheet of paper, list the titles of fiction books and short stories you've read aloud in class. Make a photocopy for each student. Ask students to cut apart the titles, rank them from most liked to least liked, and glue them in order onto another sheet of paper. Then have students share their lists in small groups, compare results, and discuss what criteria they used to make their decisions.

Model

Read "No Hoods in Class" on page 56 aloud. Then model how to complete the accompanying graphic organizer (page 57) and use it to summarize the reading selection.

Practice

Have students use a copy of the blank graphic organizer on page 58 to evaluate other fiction texts, assisting as needed.

Extend and Assess

Have students complete the related writing assignment on page 59 and one or more of the extension activities on page 60. Finally, monitor their acquisition of story evaluation by using the page 60 assessment.

Use the Graphic Organizer:

Before Reading

During Reading

✔ After Reading

No Hoods in Class

Sammy slunk into class with his sweatshirt hood pulled over his head. He slouched into his chair and opened a library book, pretending to read. "Hi, Sammy!" called Natalie as she slid into the seat beside his. Sammy scowled and sunk deeper into his chair.

The bell rang. "Good morning, class," said Mr. Peters. "Please do the writing warm-up I've listed on the board while I take attendance."

Sammy grabbed a pencil and paper from his desk and stared at the day's topic —SOMETHING YOU HIDE. *How ironic*, he thought. He began to write and jumped as the teacher touched his shoulder. "You know what the school handbook says," said Mr. Peters. "No hoods in class. Please hang your sweatshirt in your locker, Sammy—or at least pull the hood down off your head."

"I can't," whispered Sammy.

"You can't?" asked Mr. Peters. "Why not?"

"Because . . . I gave myself . . . a haircut last night," stammered Sammy. "It looks awful. It's all . . . spiky. I'm embarrassed."

"I see," said Mr. Peters. "I had the same problem once when I was your age. Luckily we didn't have the hood rule back then. But now we do, so you'll have to decide whether to follow it or go to the office."

Sammy groaned. "I'll take it off," he said. "I guess if everyone laughs, everyone laughs."

Just then, Justin ran into the room. "Sorry I'm late Mr. Peters," he called. "I got this cool new haircut after school yesterday. My dad paid the barber $30, but it took me forever to get it spiked just right this morning."

Sammy grinned and pulled off his hood. "My hair looks just like yours, and I cut it myself," he said triumphantly.

"Cool!" said Natalie and Justin.

"Maybe you should have your own barbershop when you grow up," said Mr. Peters. "Now, class, about that writing warm-up. . . ."

Reading Selection Title ___No Hoods in Class___

Answer the following questions to record your feelings and opinions about the story.

_____ **I like this story.** ☺ __X__ **This story is okay.** 😐 _____ **I don't like this story.** ☹	**Why?** I can relate to Sammy because I cut my own hair when I was really little. I don't remember it, but my Mom has pictures!
My favorite part of the story is . . . when Sammy discovers that he and Justin have the same haircut.	**Why?** I like surprises in a story, and that surprised me. It's funny, too, but I think it might be too much of a coincidence to make the story believable.
My least favorite part of the story is . . . when Mr. Peters has to come to Sammy's desk to remind him about the school rules.	**Why?** I wouldn't like to be in that situation.
I'd like to ask the author . . . if this is a true story or if the author made it up.	**Why?** If it's true, I'd like to know who it happened to. If the author made it up, I'd like to know where she or he got the idea.
___My sister___ **might like to read this story.**	**Why?** She's working on "show, don't tell" in her writing class, so she'd like the first paragraph where the author describes how Sammy feels without coming right out and saying it.

Now use your graphic organizer to summarize the reading selection to a partner.

Name _____ **Date** _____

Reading Selection Title _____

Answer the following questions to record your feelings and opinions about the story.

_____ **I like this story.** ☺ _____ **This story is okay.** 😐 _____ **I don't like this story.** ☹	**Why?**
My favorite part of the story is . . .	**Why?**
My least favorite part of the story is . . .	**Why?**
I'd like to ask the author . . .	**Why?**
_____ **might like to read this story.**	**Why?**

Now use your graphic organizer to summarize the reading selection to a partner.

Name _____   **Date** _____

Use the graphic organizer to evaluate a brief fiction selection. Then ask a classmate to do the same and write a paragraph comparing your responses.

_____

_____

_____

_____

_____

_____

_____

_____

_____

_____

_____

_____

_____

_____

_____

Extension Activities

Have students:

- write their own stories about a time they wanted to hide and then share them with partners or in small groups and evaluate one another's work.

- discuss how they select fiction books to read. The title? The author? The art? The book-jacket blurb? Then give an example of a time a book didn't measure up to their expectations.

- discuss the following statement: *A book is like a friend.*

- make a chart listing different ways they can share their book evaluations, such as drawing a poster, putting on a skit, or writing a letter to the author.

- use the graphic organizer to evaluate an episode of a favorite sitcom viewed at home and then share it with the class.

- use the graphic organizer to evaluate a poem.

Strategy Assessment

Have students sketch their own story evaluation graphic organizers on notebook paper. Locate a brief, interesting story from a grade-appropriate magazine or anthology. Read it aloud slowly, pausing periodically so students can record information on their graphic organizers. If needed, read it once more at a quicker pace so students can check their work.

Conduct one-on-one or small-group conferences to review students' graphic organizers, clarify any confusion, and answer any questions they still have about the strategy. Use this information to plan additional instruction, if needed, along with opportunities for periodic review and practice.

Connecting with Stories

Good readers constantly relate the characters, settings, and events of stories to their own lives, prior knowledge, and personal experiences. For example: *The main character has an older brother. I do, too—sometimes we get along and sometimes we don't. This story takes place near the ocean. I've been to an ocean—I can almost hear the waves crashing on the shore. In the last soccer story I read, the team won at the end. Here the team loses, but they still know they did their best.* This type of purposeful, active engagement with stories helps readers enjoy them more, understand them better, and remember them longer.

Introduce the Strategy

Locate a library book related to baby-sitters, such as *Amelia Bedelia and the Baby* by Peggy Parrish or a selection from the Baby-Sitters Club series by Ann M. Martin. Display the book and write the word *baby-sitter* on the board. Divide the class into small groups. First, have the groups discuss their personal experiences with baby-sitters (or being baby-sitters). Next, have them tell what they know about baby-sitters, such as how they can obtain training from the American Red Cross, what parents expect of them, or how much they are paid. Finally, have students share any books or stories they've read that include a baby-sitter. Explain that effective readers make these types of connections before, during, and after reading in order to get the most out of a story.

Model

Read "Sandia Peak" on page 62 aloud. Then model how to complete the accompanying graphic organizer (page 63) and use it to summarize the reading selection.

Practice

Have students use a copy of the blank graphic organizer on page 64 to make connections in other fiction texts, assisting as needed.

Extend and Assess

Have students complete the related writing assignment on page 65 and one or more of the extension activities on page 66. Finally, monitor their acquisition of making connections by using the page 66 assessment.

Use the Graphic Organizer:

✔ Before Reading
✔ During Reading
✔ After Reading

Sandia Peak

"What a cool, pleasant autumn day," said Aunt Sophia. "See the sun coming up? I've waited fifteen years to make this trek . . . since before you were born. I'm glad you grew up enough to come with me!"

Zachary grinned as he looked over the edge of the tram that slowly ascended Sandia Peak. "How long will it take us to walk back down the mountain?" he asked.

"The guide I talked to said eight hours," said Aunt Sophia. "That's why we're getting such an early start. And that's why we wore our sturdiest shoes and brought our backpacks and water bottles. It will be a long, but glorious day."

The ride up Sandia Peak was an adventure itself. The tram chugged quietly along. First Zachary observed the tell-tale signs of civilization, including busy parking lots and bustling sight-seers. However, these were soon replaced by colorful shrubs and wildflowers. Pine trees sprouted cones bigger than his fist. Occasionally he glimpsed a squirrel, deer, or raccoon. A hawk flew lazily overhead, and canyon wrens fluttered about, singing to one another.

As they neared the top, the aspens were in full fall color. The leaves sparkled in the sunlight, flicking shades of red and orange about the tram. The slight breeze caused them to rustle a little tune. "I almost wish the ride wouldn't end," said Aunt Sophia with a sigh.

"I see the Visitor Center!" called Zachary as the tram pulled to a sudden stop. He and Aunt Sophia went inside to locate their hiking guide. They listened to the detailed instructions and checked out their gear. They made sure their shoelaces were tight and their backpacks were balanced. Then they double-checked to make sure their water bottles were filled and joined the group gathering at the exit.

"I forgot to tell you something," said Zachary as they took their first steps down the mountain. "I looked up 'Sandia Peak' on the Internet. I learned that *Sandia* is a Spanish word for *watermelon*. I'm going to remember this day every time I eat watermelon for the rest of my life!"

"So am I," said Aunt Sophia with a laugh. "So am I!"

Reading Selection Title _Sandia Peak_

Write the title of the story. Then record connections to your own experiences, what you already know, and related fiction or nonfiction texts you've read.

My own experiences:

1. I've been hiking.

2. I have a collection of pinecones from a trip to the Rockies.

3. I once went on vacation with my grandparents.

TITLE:

Sandia Peak

What I already know:

1. The Sandia Mountains are in New Mexico.

2. Hikers need good shoes and a supply of drinking water.

3. Both kids and adults enjoy hiking in the mountains.

Related fiction or nonfiction texts I've read:

1. *My Side of the Mountain* by Jean Craighead George

2. *Climb Away: A Mountaineer's Dream* by Deborah Parks

3. *E is for Enchantment: A New Mexico Alphabet* by Helen Foster James

Now use your graphic organizer to summarize the reading selection to a partner.

Name _____ **Date** _____

Reading Selection Title _____

Write the title of the story. Then record connections to your own experiences, what you already know, and related fiction or nonfiction texts you've read.

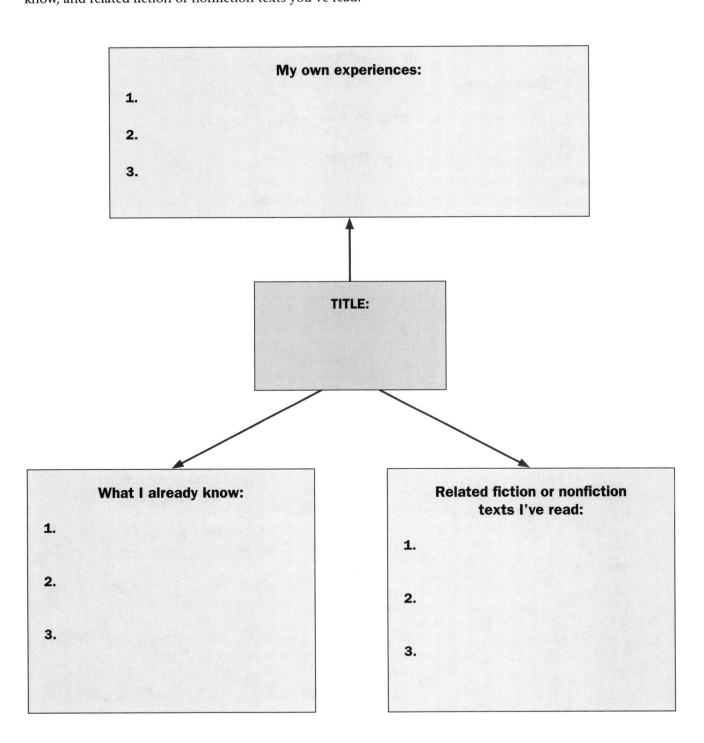

My own experiences:

1.

2.

3.

TITLE:

What I already know:

1.

2.

3.

Related fiction or nonfiction texts I've read:

1.

2.

3.

Now use your graphic organizer to summarize the reading selection to a partner.

Name _____ **Date** _____

Read a short story, and then use the graphic organizer to record related experiences, background knowledge, and texts. Write a paragraph about the connection you find most interesting.

_____

_____

_____

_____

_____

_____

_____

_____

_____

_____

_____

_____

_____

_____

Extension Activities

Have students:

- share their own stories about personal goals.

- browse the classroom library, make connections to one or more books or magazine stories, and tell the class why these connections make them eager to read the new text.

- locate and share topics in their content-area textbooks that connect to fiction books they've read.

- read each other's creative writing assignments and orally make connections.

- use the graphic organizer to make connections with a piece of art.

- use the graphic organizer to make connections with a movie.

Strategy Assessment

Have students sketch their own connections graphic organizers on notebook paper. Locate a brief, interesting story from a grade-appropriate magazine or anthology. Read it aloud slowly, pausing periodically so students can record information on their graphic organizers. If needed, read it once more at a quicker pace so students can check their work.

Conduct one-on-one or small-group conferences to review students' graphic organizers, clarify any confusion, and answer any questions they still have about the strategy. Use this information to plan additional instruction, if needed, along with opportunities for periodic review and practice.

Nonfiction Units

Surveying Text Features and Identifying the Author's Purpose

To get the most out of a nonfiction selection, careful readers first survey the text features. These include such elements as the title, table of contents, headings, subheadings, photographs, illustrations, captions, sidebars, maps, charts, graphs, diagrams, time lines, bold-faced words, vocabulary lists, glossary, and index. Readers also try to determine the author's purpose for writing the selection. For example, is the author trying to inform? Teach a new skill? Persuade? Entertain? By keeping the purpose in mind, readers can focus on the most important aspects of the text and better understand and remember what they read.

Introduce the Strategy

Hold up a science textbook. Say: *Let's pretend your science teacher just gave you a homework assignment. You're to read a chapter in the textbook and be ready to discuss the material in class tomorrow. However, you've never heard of the topic. How do you approach the reading and understand it well enough to participate in the discussion?* Have students work in small groups to discuss a solution to the problem, and then ask each group to report back to the class. Record their ideas on the chalkboard, drawing a star beside any text feature mentioned. When each group has shared, tell students they will be looking for these and other text features as you read a nonfiction selection together. Then say: *Another helpful strategy is to try to figure out why the author wrote the selection. We'll talk about that as well.*

Model

Read "Coin Games" on page 70 aloud. Then model how to complete the accompanying graphic organizer (page 71) and use it to summarize the reading selection.

Practice

Have students use a copy of the blank graphic organizer on page 72 to survey text features and identify the author's purpose in other nonfiction texts, assisting as needed.

Extend and Assess

Have students complete the related writing assignment on page 73 and one or more of the extension activities on page 74. Finally, monitor their acquisition of surveying text features and identifying author's purpose by using the page 74 assessment.

Use the Graphic Organizer:

✔ Before Reading
   During Reading
   After Reading

Coin Games

Check your pocket. Check the sofa cushions. Check the laundry hamper. Did you find a coin? If so, try these games.

Circles

Trace around your coin several times. How many different pictures can you make with the circles? A clown face? A clock? A cool pair of eyeglasses?

Drop the Coin

Put an empty can on the floor in front of you. How many tries does it take to toss in your coin? Move the can further away and try again.

Magic Trick

Cover your eyes. Ask a friend to put your coin on the table or hold it tightly for one minute and then give it to you. Guess *table* or *hand*. (**Hint:** When your friend holds the coin, it **absorbs** body heat. Say *hand* if the coin is warm. Say *table* if the coin is cold.)

Coin Toss

Toss your coin in the air 100 times. **Tally** how many times it lands on heads or tails. Try again and compare the scores.

Coin Math

What is the date on your coin? Were you born before that year? If so, figure out how much older you are than the coin. Ask friends and family members to do the same.

Collecting

Have you heard the saying, "A penny saved is a penny earned"? Put your coin in a jar. You can start saving for something special. You can also play coin games any time you like!

Glossary

absorbs—takes in
hint—clue
tally—to keep count by making marks on a paper

Reading Selection Title ___Coin Games___

Put a ✔ beside any text features you find in your reading selection. Add notes about how the text features might help you. Then write why you think the author wrote the selection.

Text Feature		Notes
title	✔	The title catches my interest. I like to play games!
table of contents		
headings	✔	The headings make it easy to tell when I'm changing from one game to the next.
subheadings		
photographs		
illustrations		
captions		
sidebars		
maps		
charts		
graphs		
diagrams		
time lines		
bold-faced words	✔	The bold-faced words remind me to check the glossary.
glossary	✔	Knowing the meanings of these words helps me understand the article better and enjoy it even more.
index		

I think the author wrote this selection to ___to teach me some fun games to play and show me how a___

___common object can be used in many different ways.___

_____

Now use your graphic organizer to summarize the reading selection to a partner.

Name _____ **Date** _____

Reading Selection Title _____

Put a ✔ beside any text features you find in your reading selection. Add notes about how the text features might help you. Then write why you think the author wrote the selection.

Text Feature		Notes
title		
table of contents		
headings		
subheadings		
photographs		
illustrations		
captions		
sidebars		
maps		
charts		
graphs		
diagrams		
time lines		
bold-faced words		
glossary		
index		

I think the author wrote this selection to _____

_____

_____

Now use your graphic organizer to summarize the reading selection to a partner.

Name _____ **Date** _____

Use the graphic organizer to record text features and the author's purpose for a topic in math, science, or social studies. Then write a paragraph about it.

_____

_____

_____

_____

_____

_____

_____

_____

_____

_____

_____

_____

_____

_____

Sample Topics:

Math: a famous mathemetician from long ago or today

Science: cave exploration

Social Studies: reading maps

Extension Activities

Have students:

- locate a book or article about collecting coins or saving money, survey the text features, and identify the author's purpose for writing the text.

- discuss the saying, "A picture is worth a thousand words" and then find and share an example from a book, newspaper, or magazine.

- locate and point out text features in their content-area textbooks.

- locate helpful text features in the directions for a board game.

- learn how to format one or more text features on a computer word-processing program.

- write a brief research paper on any topic of interest that includes three or more text features.

Strategy Assessment

Obtain a selection of short nonfiction books from the library. Have students sketch their own text feature/author's purpose graphic organizers on notebook paper. Then have each student analyze one of the books and record the results on their organizers.

Conduct one-on-one or small-group conferences to review students' graphic organizers, clarify any confusion, and answer any questions they still have about the strategy. Use this information to plan additional instruction, if needed, along with opportunities for periodic review and practice.

Building Background

Building background helps us "get ready" for a topic. First, we think about what we already know. Even better, we share and discuss our background knowledge so each of us can benefit from others' experiences. Next, we pinpoint new facts we learn about the topic from the text features. For example, do we see references to certain people, locations, events, or processes? Finally, we acquire at least one new fact about the topic before jumping in. Sometimes the teacher or another expert shares additional information. Other times, we need to do a quick bit of research in a dictionary, encyclopedia, atlas, or Web site. This helps us better visualize what we're about to read and sets the stage for successful comprehension.

Introduce the Strategy

Before class, create a greeting card for an imaginary child. The front should say, "Sorry you have chicken pox!" and show a child with spots all over his or her face. The inside should say, "Get well soon!" and be signed. Before displaying the card, say: *A child received a greeting card when he had chicken pox. What do you know about chicken pox?* Then display and read the card. Ask: *What do the text features tell you about chicken pox?* After discussion, ask: *Is chicken pox still common? Has someone invented a chicken pox vaccine? Does a person who gets chicken pox after being vaccinated have a milder case of the disease? Do you know? Let's look that up on a medical Web site to find out.* Demonstrate a quick search on a medical Web site such as www.cdc.gov to find answers to these questions. Then explain that this background knowledge helps you understand more about the card. For example, it was likely sent to a child a few years ago rather than today.

Model

Read "Penguin Parade" on page 76 aloud. Then model how to complete the accompanying graphic organizer (page 77) and use it to summarize the reading selection.

Practice

Have students use a copy of the blank graphic organizer on page 78 to build background in other nonfiction texts, assisting as needed.

Extend and Assess

Have students complete the related writing assignment on page 79 and one or more of the extension activities on page 80. Finally, monitor their acquisition of building background by using the page 80 assessment.

Use the Graphic Organizer:

✔ Before Reading
  During Reading
  After Reading

Penguin Parade

Every year, half a million people go to a tiny island. At sunset, they hold their breath. They see the water churning just off the shore. They hear a strange call. Then they see tiny feathered heads. The animals scan the beach for danger. One by one, they hit the shallow water. They waddle ashore and head for their burrows. Soon, they're safely tucked in for the night. The people clap their hands as the penguin parade comes to an end.

Phillip Island, Australia

The Phillip Island penguins are only twelve inches tall. Their scientific name is *Eudyptala minor*, which means "good little diver." However, they are usually called *fairy penguins* or *little blues*. Although they can also be found in other coastal spots around Australia, they seem to thrive in the Phillip Island Nature Park. The penguins are one of the most famous attractions in the country.

Oil Spill!

On New Year's Day in 2000, an oil spill occurred near Phillip Island. Scientists needed to keep the penguins from picking at their feathers so they wouldn't swallow any oil. Someone designed a sweater knitted of wool. It had tiny slits in the sides for the penguins' flippers. The pattern was posted on a Web site, and knitters around the world came to the rescue. The Nature Park received thousands of sweaters. Now they sell toy penguins wearing the sweaters in the gift shop. People who visit the real penguin parade can buy a fun memento to help them remember the show.

Reading Selection Title _Penguin Parade_

Record what you already know about the topic, what you learn from the text features, and what you discover through a brief, initial research.

I already knew . . .	The text features told me . . .	To help me better understand the text, I found out that . . .
Penguins only live in certain parts of the world. Most of them are black and white. They like to swim, and they waddle when they walk.	The penguins in this article live on Phillip Island, Australia.	**Source:** _atlas_ Phillip Island is off the southern coast of Australia near Melbourne.
	The penguins were affected by an oil spill.	**Source:** _online encyclopedia_ An oil spill happens when oil accidentally leaks out of a tanker ship or underwater pipeline. The oily water hurts or kills many ocean plants and animals. First, workers try to keep the oil from spreading. Then they clean it up.

Now use your graphic organizer to summarize the reading selection to a partner.

Name _____   **Date** _____

Reading Selection Title _____

Record what you already know about the topic, what you learn from the text features, and what you discover through a brief, initial research.

I already knew . . .	The text features told me . . .	To help me better understand the text, I found out that . . .
		Source: _____ **Source:** _____

Now use your graphic organizer to summarize the reading selection to a partner.

Name _____ **Date** _____

Use the graphic organizer to record background information about a math, science, or social studies topic you'd like to learn more about. When you're through, write a paragraph about what you know.

_____

_____

_____

_____

_____

_____

_____

_____

_____

_____

_____

_____

_____

_____

Sample Topics:

Math: geometry in day-to-day life
Science: inventions that might allow us to travel to other planets someday
Social Studies: holidays other countries share with the United States

Extension Activities

Have students:

- use the information in "Penguin Parade" as background knowledge for reading another article about penguins, Australia, or oil spills.

- make a list of "kid-friendly" Web sites where they can get quick bits of information, such as www.factmonster.com.

- use the graphic organizer to build background before reading a new chapter in a content-area textbook.

- record their background knowledge on a topic with sketches rather than words.

- use the graphic organizer to build background about an upcoming guest speaker.

- share their completed graphic organizers with partners to boost and affirm each other's prior knowledge about a topic.

Strategy Assessment

Obtain a selection of short nonfiction books from the library. Have students sketch their own building background graphic organizers on notebook paper. Then have each student analyze one of the books, look up further information, and record the results on his or her organizer.

Conduct one-on-one or small-group conferences to review students' graphic organizers, clarify any confusion, and answer any questions they still have about the strategy. Use this information to plan additional instruction, if needed, along with opportunities for periodic review and practice.

Asking Questions and Setting a Purpose for Reading

When you go grocery shopping, you take a list. This helps you stay focused and come out of the store with the items you need most. A similar strategy is asking questions and setting a purpose for reading. When we begin a reading selection knowing what we want to get out of it, we're able to focus on the most important information. As a result, we better understand what we read as we move through the text and better remember key details when we're finished.

Introduce the Strategy

Pair students and tell them they will interview one another. Ask: *What do you want to find out about your classmate? Are you interested in learning about his or her family? Hobbies? Favorite movies? Pets? Pet peeves?* Have students list at least three questions to ask. Then say: *Now write down your purpose for the interview to help you stay on track. For example, do you want to get to know your classmate better? Do you want to find things you have in common? Do you want to get ideas for new activities to try?* After students have completed their interviews, allow them to report back to the class. Ask: *Did you learn the answers to your questions? Did you successfully accomplish the purpose of the interview? Why or why not?*

Model

Read "The Sandy Hook Lighthouse" on page 82 aloud. Then model how to complete the accompanying graphic organizer (page 83) and use it to summarize the reading selection.

Practice

Have students use a copy of the blank graphic organizer on page 84 to ask questions and set a purpose for reading other nonfiction texts, assisting as needed.

Extend and Assess

Have students complete the related writing assignment on page 85 and one or more of the extension activities on page 86. Finally, monitor their acquisition of this strategy by using the page 86 assessment.

Use the Graphic Organizer:

✔ Before Reading
✔ During Reading
✔ After Reading

The Sandy Hook Lighthouse

In America's early years, the sound of a crashing ship was common. Captains couldn't see where they were at night. They had to guess whether their ships were close to land.

Lighthouses helped solve this problem. The first one, Sandy Hook, was built in 1764. It sits on a piece of land near New York Harbor. The lighthouse has eight sides and thick walls. It has survived terrible weather and three wars.

The first lantern in the tower had two candles. These were not like candles you may use in your home. They were made of whale oil poured into a pan and topped with twenty-four wicks. The pans were then hung from the ceiling. The lanterns burned all night to light the harbor.

A keeper lived at the lighthouse. He lit the candles every night and snuffed them out in the mornings. Then the keeper trimmed the wicks, filled the oil, and cleaned the soot off the walls.

Later, Sandy Hook's candles were replaced by oil lamps. In the 1850s, new lenses made the lights brighter. Crewmen on ships could see them miles away. Today the lighthouse uses electricity.

Sandy Hook Lighthouse is now part of the Gateway National Recreation Area in New Jersey. The Coast Guard takes care of the light. The tower and keeper's house look like new. Visitors are welcome during the spring and summer months. Perhaps you can go someday!

Reading Selection Title   The Sandy Hook Lighthouse

Before reading, write the topic, your questions about the topic, and your purpose for reading the text. During reading, write the answers to your questions and add more questions that come to mind. After reading, finish answering the questions and write whether or not you accomplished your purpose.

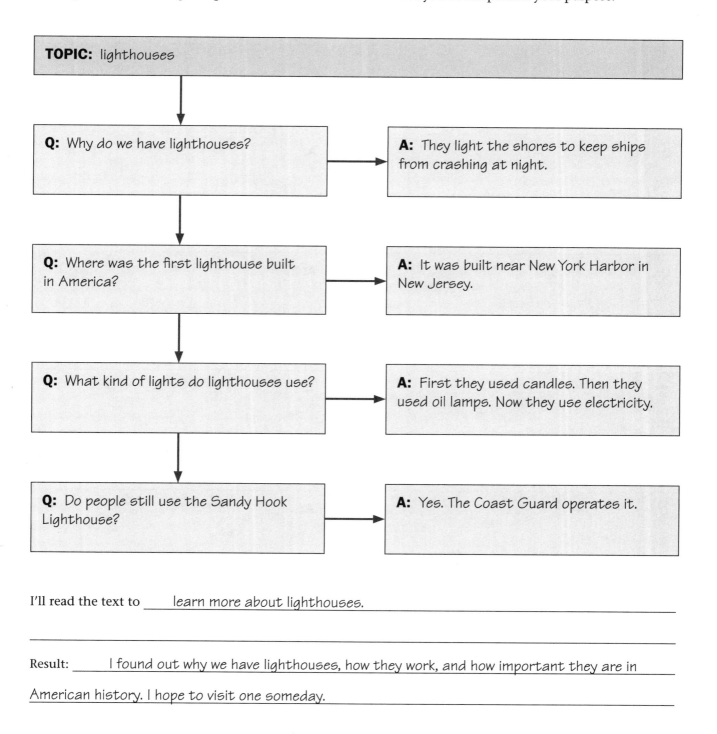

TOPIC: lighthouses

Q: Why do we have lighthouses?

A: They light the shores to keep ships from crashing at night.

Q: Where was the first lighthouse built in America?

A: It was built near New York Harbor in New Jersey.

Q: What kind of lights do lighthouses use?

A: First they used candles. Then they used oil lamps. Now they use electricity.

Q: Do people still use the Sandy Hook Lighthouse?

A: Yes. The Coast Guard operates it.

I'll read the text to   learn more about lighthouses.

Result: I found out why we have lighthouses, how they work, and how important they are in American history. I hope to visit one someday.

Now use your graphic organizer to summarize the reading selection to a partner.

Name _____ **Date** _____

Reading Selection Title _____

Before reading, write the topic, your questions about the topic, and your purpose for reading the text. During reading, write the answers to your questions and add more questions that come to mind. After reading, finish answering the questions and write whether or not you accomplished your purpose.

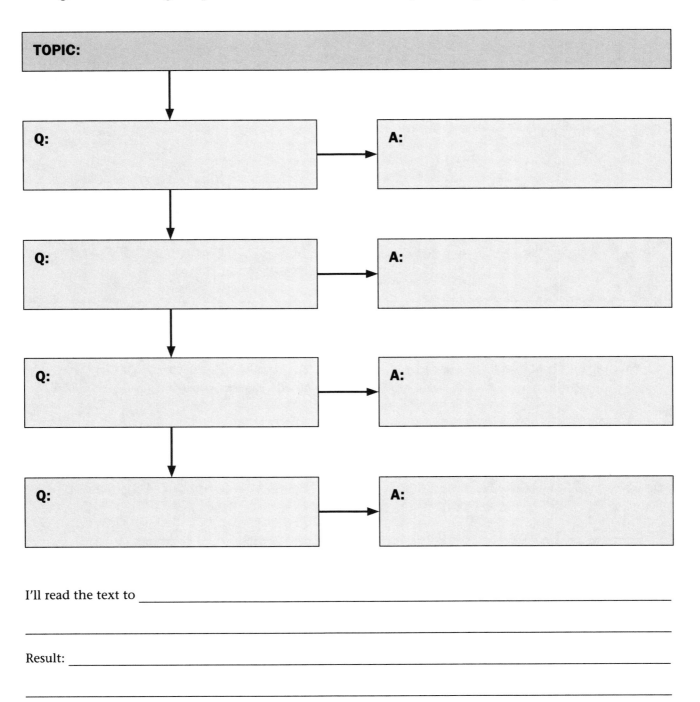

I'll read the text to _____

_____

Result: _____

_____

Now use your graphic organizer to summarize the reading selection to a partner.

Name _____ **Date** _____

Use the graphic organizer to record questions and set a purpose for reading a brief math, science, or social studies article. Then read the article and write a paragraph that answers your questions.

_____

_____

_____

_____

_____

_____

_____

_____

_____

_____

_____

_____

_____

Sample Topics:

Math: a math career

Science: plants that grow in your area

Social Studies: Native Americans who settled your area long ago

Extension Activities

Have students:

- use the graphic organizer to ask questions and set a purpose for reading another article about early safety inventions.

- look through their content-area textbooks and find places where the authors directly state the purpose for reading a certain unit, chapter, or section.

- discuss how and where to find answers to questions that aren't answered in a text selection.

- use the graphic organizer to plan an interview with an adult about his or her career.

- use the graphic organizer to ask questions and set a purpose for watching a content-area video in class.

- use the graphic organizer before and after listening to a nonfiction book on tape.

Strategy Assessment

Have students sketch their own questions/purpose graphic organizers on notebook paper. Locate a brief, interesting article on a topic of your choice. Read the title aloud. If the title doesn't indicate what the article is about, provide a one-sentence summary. Allow time for students to fill in the before-reading sections of the graphic organizer. Then read the article aloud and have students complete their organizers.

Conduct one-on-one or small-group conferences to review students' graphic organizers, clarify any confusion, and answer any questions they still have about the strategy. Use this information to plan additional instruction, if needed, along with opportunities for periodic review and practice.

Drawing Conclusions

Pretend you're reading a biography about a famous pianist. At various points in the text you read that (1) she begged to take piano lessons at age three, (2) she routinely practiced three to four hours a day while other children played outside, and (3) while growing up she offered to perform for everyone who stopped by the house—even the mailman. The author doesn't have to state that this pianist was precocious, outgoing, and dedicated to her craft. You, as the reader, can draw these conclusions on your own. Drawing conclusions means applying what you already know about the world to evidence in a text and arriving at a logical outcome. Because effective authors know that readers like to reason and think critically for themselves, they are careful to provide enough—but not too much—information about the topic at hand.

Introduce the Strategy

Hand out slips of paper with the headings "Hobby," "Favorite Book," and "Dreams for the Future" and ask students to fill in each category about themselves. Then collect the papers, mix them up, and place them facedown on a table. Have students take turns selecting a list and reading it aloud while the rest of the group uses the clues to conclude which classmate is being described. Remind students to apply what they already know about the people in the class to the evidence they hear. When everyone is done, discuss the experience and have students tell a partner how this skill might be applied to reading.

Model

Read "'Killer' Whales" on page 88 aloud. Then model how to complete the accompanying graphic organizer (page 89) and use it to summarize the reading selection.

Practice

Have students use a copy of the blank graphic organizer on page 90 to draw conclusions in other nonfiction texts, assisting as needed.

Extend and Assess

Have students complete the related writing assignment on page 91 and one or more of the extension activities on page 92. Finally, monitor their acquisition of drawing conclusions by using the page 92 assessment.

Use the Graphic Organizer:

Before Reading
✔ During Reading
✔ After Reading

"Killer Whales"

Long ago, Spanish whale hunters had helpers in the sea. First the helpers led them to large whales. Then they collaborated in the capture and kill. As a reward, the whalers threw the tongues of the whales they caught to their assistants—a favorite treat.

Who were these helpers? Although the Spanish whalers called them *whale killers*, many people call them *killer whales* today. Scientists call them *orcas*.

Orcas are found in oceans all over the world. Females may reach a length of fifteen feet, and males may be thirty feet long. They have black backs, white bellies, and white oval patches around their eyes.

Their high dorsal fins are triangular and their flippers are shaped like paddles. They have more than four dozen razor-sharp teeth with which to feed on sea mammals, birds, and fish, and they have no natural enemies—including sharks.

Because of the orcas' size, appearance, and turned-around nickname, most people think they kill human beings. However, orcas have never been known to hunt a man, woman, or child. Sadly, we haven't returned the favor. The biggest threat to a killer whale is a human.

Reading Selection Title _____ "Killer" Whales _____

Record information that helps you draw conclusions about the topic. Label the information **TE** for *text evidence* and **BK** for *background knowledge*.

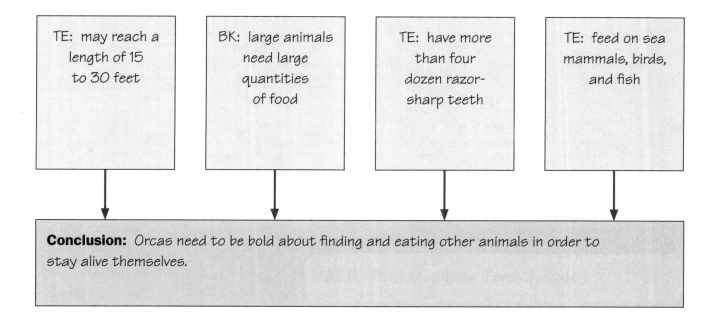

TE: may reach a length of 15 to 30 feet

BK: large animals need large quantities of food

TE: have more than four dozen razor-sharp teeth

TE: feed on sea mammals, birds, and fish

Conclusion: Orcas need to be bold about finding and eating other animals in order to stay alive themselves.

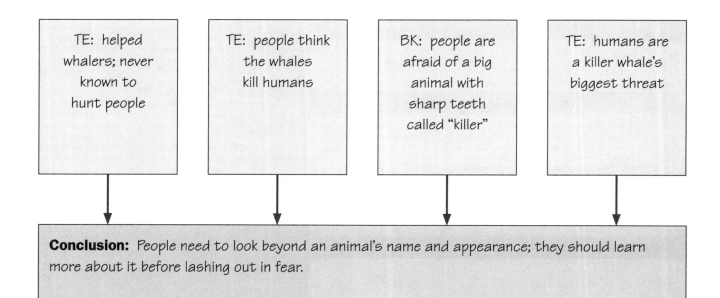

TE: helped whalers; never known to hunt people

TE: people think the whales kill humans

BK: people are afraid of a big animal with sharp teeth called "killer"

TE: humans are a killer whale's biggest threat

Conclusion: People need to look beyond an animal's name and appearance; they should learn more about it before lashing out in fear.

Now use your graphic organizer to summarize the reading selection to a partner.

Name _____ **Date** _____

Reading Selection Title _____

Record information that helps you draw conclusions about the topic. Label the information
TE for *text evidence* and **BK** for *background knowledge*.

Conclusion:

Conclusion:

Now use your graphic organizer to summarize the reading selection to a partner.

Name _____ **Date** _____

Use the graphic organizer to draw conclusions about a topic you've studied in math, science, or social studies. Then write a paragraph about it.

_____

_____

_____

_____

_____

_____

_____

_____

_____

_____

_____

_____

_____

_____

_____

_____

Sample Topics:

Math: probability

Science: animal adaptations

Social Studies: world hunger

Extension Activities

Have students:

• repeat the introductory activity using new criteria.

• use the graphic organizer to draw conclusions in another article about an unusual animal.

• share conclusions they draw from their content-area textbooks.

• think of examples in which people could draw the wrong conclusion despite applying prior knowledge to substantial evidence.

• find examples of titles in a newspaper or magazine that draw a conclusion about the information stated in the accompanying article.

• locate a picture of an unusual painting, sculpture, or photograph and use the graphic organizer to draw a conclusion about the artist.

Strategy Assessment

As students sketch their own drawing conclusions graphic organizers on notebook paper, write the following statements on the board. Have students analyze them for text evidence, call up their prior knowledge, and record the results on their graphic organizers.

• The blue whale is the largest animal in the world. Adults can reach one hundred feet long. Not even a dinosaur skeleton is this large.

• The blue whale is the loudest animal in the world. People from hundreds of miles away can hear its call.

• Blue whales can live one hundred years or more. However, because of whalers, they are now listed as an endangered species.

Conduct one-on-one or small-group conferences to review students' graphic organizers, clarify any confusion, and answer any questions they still have about the strategy. Use this information to plan additional instruction, if needed, along with opportunities for periodic review and practice.

Identifying Main Idea and Supporting Details

When reading a nonfiction passage, readers need to identify the most important point the author makes. This main idea may relate to a section, chapter, or the whole text. By locating details that go with or tell something about the main idea and recognizing those that do not relate, readers are able to understand and remember the information more easily. Often the author explicitly states the main idea at the beginning or end of the reading selection. Other times the main idea is not so easily identifiable and readers must figure out on their own what the author considers most important. Identifying main idea and supporting details is an especially useful strategy for summarizing.

Introduce the Strategy

Put students in pairs. Have one partner talk about a topic for one to two minutes while the other partner takes notes. After the time is up, ask the partners to look at the notes and try to identify the speaker's main idea and any details that support it. The partners then switch roles with a new topic. After everyone has had a turn, invite partners to share a main idea or supporting detail with the class and tell why it was important. Possible topics are: *the most important subject at school, whether kids should get after-school jobs, an ideal menu for the school lunchroom, household chores all kids should learn to do, an activity that helps kids learn leadership skills, an animal that makes a good pet,* or *what I know about _____.*

Model

Read "Run for the Roses" on page 94 aloud. Then model how to complete the accompanying graphic organizer (page 95) and use it to summarize the reading selection.

Practice

Have students use a copy of the blank graphic organizer on page 96 to identify the main idea and supporting details in other nonfiction texts, assisting as needed.

Extend and Assess

Have students complete the related writing assignment on page 97 and one or more of the extension activities on page 98. Finally, monitor their acquisition of main idea/supporting details identification by using the page 98 assessment.

Use the Graphic Organizer:

Before Reading

✔ During Reading

✔ After Reading

Run for the Roses

The family gathers around the television. The neighbors knock on the door and are welcomed into the room. A platter of cheese, meat, and chips with dip appears on the coffee table. Everyone gets a can of soda and finds a comfortable seat. It's the first Saturday in May, time for the Kentucky Derby.

The Kentucky Derby is a famous horse race held in Louisville each year. In 1924, a horse named Black Gold seemed a likely loser as he ran in sixth place. However, as the horses reached the backstretch, Black Gold broke away from the pack. A half-length ahead of the second-place horse, Black Gold won the Derby.

Black Gold's owner was a widowed Native American woman named Rosa Hoots. She was so proud of Black Gold that she draped his back with a blanket of roses she had made. Little did Mrs. Hoots know that her reward for the horse would start a tradition.

A radio announcer describing the event gave the Kentucky Derby a new nickname. To this day, the Kentucky Derby is known as "The Run for the Roses." The winning horse is still presented with a blanket of roses, too.

Reading Selection Title   Run for the Roses

Write important details from each paragraph. Then use them to determine the main idea for the selection. Or, if the main idea is stated first, write it down and then record the details that go with it.

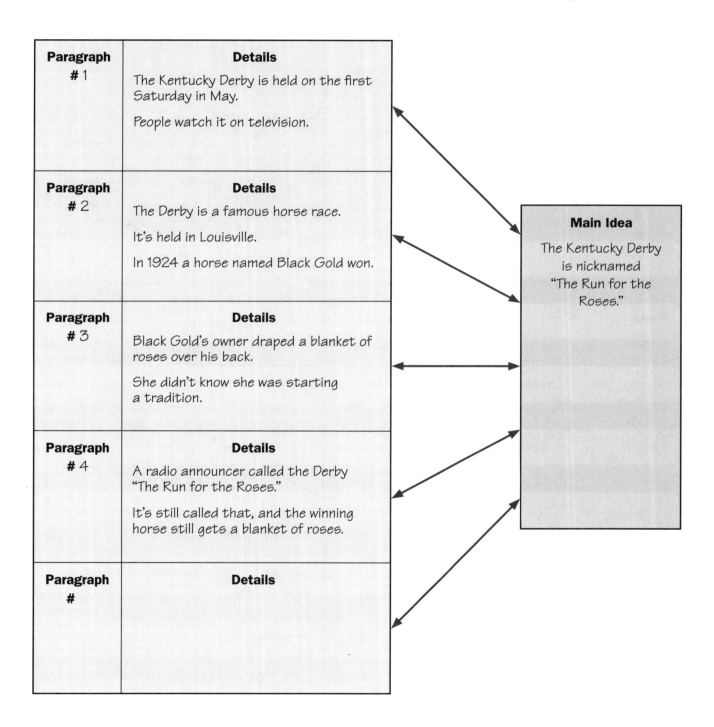

Paragraph #1	**Details** The Kentucky Derby is held on the first Saturday in May. People watch it on television.
Paragraph #2	**Details** The Derby is a famous horse race. It's held in Louisville. In 1924 a horse named Black Gold won.
Paragraph #3	**Details** Black Gold's owner draped a blanket of roses over his back. She didn't know she was starting a tradition.
Paragraph #4	**Details** A radio announcer called the Derby "The Run for the Roses." It's still called that, and the winning horse still gets a blanket of roses.
Paragraph #	**Details**

Main Idea

The Kentucky Derby is nicknamed "The Run for the Roses."

Now use your graphic organizer to summarize the reading selection to a partner.

Name _____ **Date** _____

Reading Selection Title _____

Write important details from each paragraph. Then use them to determine the main idea for the selection. Or, if the main idea is stated first, write it down and then record the details that go with it.

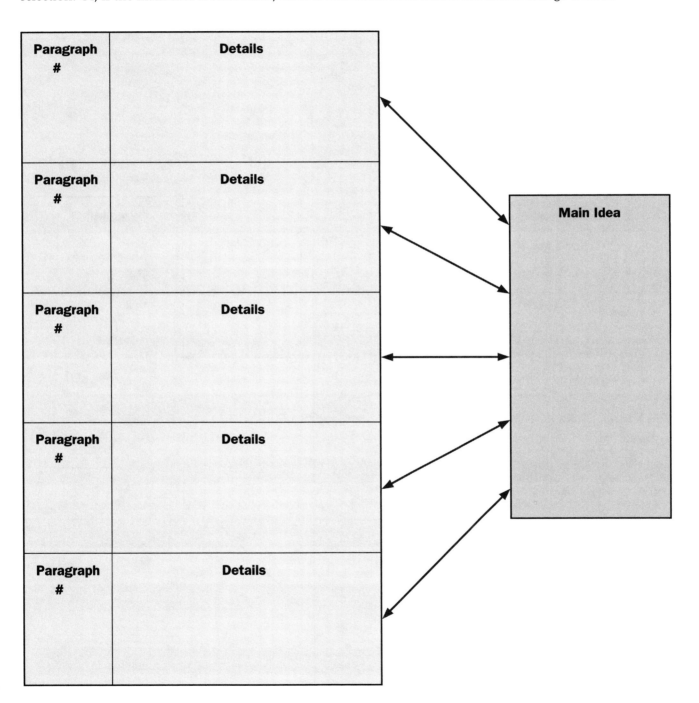

Paragraph #	Details
Paragraph #	Details
Paragraph #	Details
Paragraph #	Details
Paragraph #	Details

Main Idea

Now use your graphic organizer to summarize the reading selection to a partner.

Name _____ **Date** _____

Use the graphic organizer to record the main idea and supporting details of a topic you've studied in math, science, or social studies. Then write a paragraph about it.

_____

_____

_____

_____

_____

_____

_____

_____

_____

_____

_____

_____

_____

_____

_____

Sample Topics:

Math: prime numbers

Science: subway systems

Social Studies: time zones in the United States

Extension Activities

Have students:

- revisit the completed graphic organizer on page 95 and cross off any details that don't add to the main idea.

- use the graphic organizer to record the main idea and supporting details in another article about a famous horse race.

- locate and share a main idea and supporting details from a content-area textbook.

- make a list of various ways authors organize supporting details, such as describing an event in time order, giving reasons from least important to most important, or describing an object from top to bottom.

- use the graphic organizer to record the main idea and supporting details as they watch a content-area video in class.

- use the graphic organizer to record the "main idea" and "supporting details" in a famous art reproduction.

Strategy Assessment

Have students sketch their own main idea/supporting details graphic organizers on notebook paper. Locate a brief, interesting article on a topic of your choice. Read it aloud slowly, pausing periodically so students can record information on their graphic organizers. If needed, read it once more at a quicker pace so students can check their work.

Conduct one-on-one or small-group conferences to review students' graphic organizers, clarify any confusion, and answer any questions they still have about the strategy. Use this information to plan additional instruction, if needed, along with opportunities for periodic review and practice.

Examining Descriptions

When we read, we create a mental picture of the people, places, objects, and actions described. Sometimes the author appeals to all the senses—sight, sound, taste, smell, and touch. Other times, fewer senses apply. Sometimes the author arranges the details in a specific order, such as top to bottom or front to back. Other times, the portrayal is random. Regardless of the organization, allowing ourselves to "experience" these descriptions helps us become more involved with what we're reading, utilize our prior knowledge, and better understand the relationships between ideas in the text.

Introduce the Strategy

Place several common objects into separate small, brown paper bags and fold over the tops. Number the bags clearly on the outside. Explain that students are allowed to feel, smell, and listen to the bags but not look inside. Pass out the bags, allowing time for examination, and then have each student record the bag's number on a slip of paper along with a guess about the contents. Next, have students exchange bags and repeat the process. When everyone has guessed at several items, collect the bags. Read a bag number and ask: *Who had this number? What do you think the object is? Why do you think so?* Then remove the item from the bag so students can check their guesses. Continue until all the items are displayed.

Model

Read "Name That Snake!" on page 100 aloud. Then model how to complete the accompanying graphic organizer (page 101) and use it to summarize the reading selection.

Practice

Have students use a copy of the blank graphic organizer on page 102 to examine descriptions in other nonfiction texts, assisting as needed.

Extend and Assess

Have students complete the related writing assignment on page 103 and one or more of the extension activities on page 104. Finally, monitor their acquisition of description examination by using the page 104 assessment.

Use the Graphic Organizer:

Before Reading
✔ During Reading
After Reading

Name That Snake!

It's twenty feet long. It's found in the tropics of Africa, Asia, Australia, and the South Pacific islands. It has sharp fangs but isn't poisonous. It can climb and swim. What is it? A python!

Pythons belong to the boa family. Boa family snakes are constrictors—they silently creep up and squeeze their prey to death before eating it. Boas are smaller than pythons and live mostly in North, Central, and South America. They bear live young, whereas pythons lay eggs.

Another snake in the boa family is the South American anaconda. Only the royal python rivals the anaconda in size. Both may reach a length of thirty feet. The royal python is found in the towns and forests of Southeast Asia, Indonesia, and the Philippines.

Constrictors have many physical traits in common. For example, they all have thick bodies. Their flat heads are shaped like rectangles. Their varying colors help them hide, and they're able to open their mouths wide enough to swallow animals whole.

Now do some research on your own. Learn about a snake from another family, such as colubrid, pit viper, or cobra. Write some clues, and ask a friend to play "Name That Snake!"

Reading Selection Title ___Name That Snake!___

As you read the selection, record details you can *see, hear, taste, smell,* and *touch.*

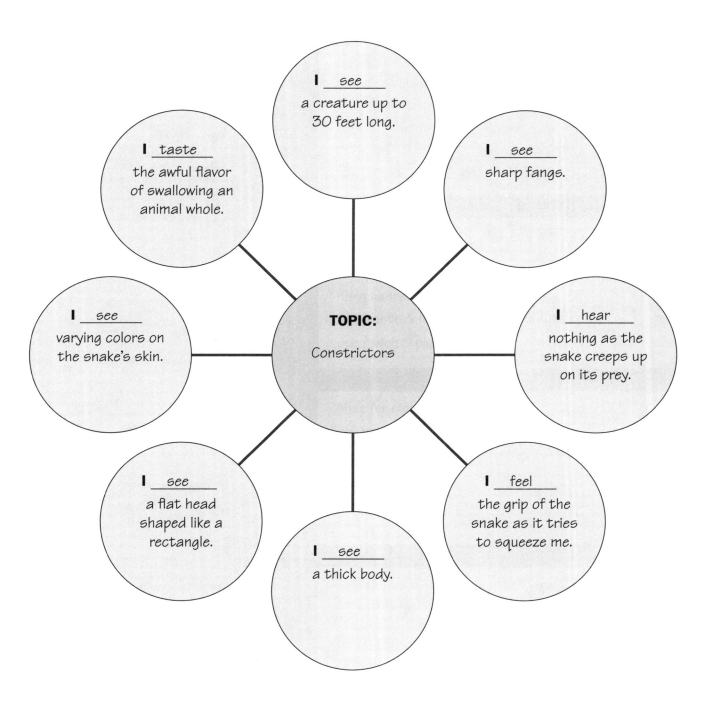

I ___see___
a creature up to
30 feet long.

I ___see___
sharp fangs.

I ___taste___
the awful flavor
of swallowing an
animal whole.

I ___hear___
nothing as the
snake creeps up
on its prey.

I ___see___
varying colors on
the snake's skin.

TOPIC:
Constrictors

I ___feel___
the grip of the
snake as it tries
to squeeze me.

I ___see___
a flat head
shaped like a
rectangle.

I ___see___
a thick body.

Now use your graphic organizer to summarize the reading selection to a partner.

Name _____ **Date** _____

Reading Selection Title _____

As you read the selection, record details you can *see, hear, taste, smell,* and *touch.*

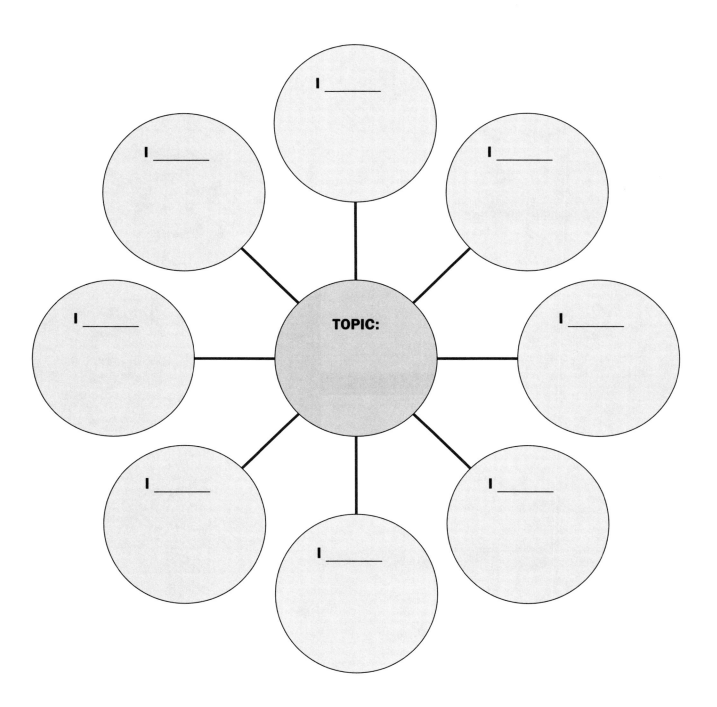

Now use your graphic organizer to summarize the reading selection to a partner.

Name _____ **Date** _____

Use the graphic organizer to examine descriptions in a topic you've studied in math, science, or social studies. Then write a paragraph about it.

_____

_____

_____

_____

_____

_____

_____

_____

_____

_____

_____

_____

_____

_____

_____

Sample Topics:

Math: a three-dimensional geometric shape
Science: an unusual animal
Social Studies: a famous landmark in your state

Extension Activities

Have students:

- use the graphic organizer to record descriptive features of other kinds of snakes and then play "Name That Snake!" with classmates.

- take turns calling out different settings while classmates record what they might see, hear, smell, touch, and taste in each one.

- locate and share descriptions from their content-area textbooks.

- cut out interesting pictures from old newspapers and magazines and use the graphic organizer to record descriptive details.

- bring a mystery item (or photo of an item) from home, use the graphic organizer to describe it, have classmates use the clues to guess the name of the item, and then reveal it.

- make a collage of newspaper headlines that contain descriptions readers can see, hear, smell, touch, or taste.

Strategy Assessment

As students sketch their own description graphic organizers on notebook paper, write the following statements on the board. Have students analyze them and record the results on their graphic organizers.

- The poisonous copperhead snake may reach a length of four feet.

- Its back is brown with colored crossbands, its belly is pinkish-white with spots, and its head is a pale copper color.

- Many people think copperheads have a cucumber-like aroma.

- They eat small mammals, large insects, frogs, and other snakes.

- Copperheads are afraid of humans but will strike if startled or attacked.

- If one bites you, you will experience severe pain and illness but probably recover.

Conduct one-on-one or small-group conferences to review students' graphic organizers, clarify any confusion, and answer any questions they still have about the strategy. Use this information to plan additional instruction, if needed, along with opportunities for periodic review and practice.

Analyzing Cause and Effect

An action with a result is called a cause-and-effect relationship. The effect is *what* happens, and the cause is *why* it happens. One cause can have several effects. Additionally, an effect can cause a new action to occur. Identifying cause and effect helps us connect information in order to better understand what we read. Some common cause-and-effect cue words and phrases are *because, so, therefore, subsequently, due to, consequently, if/then, as a result, when, caused, for, which led to, resulting from, effect, in order to,* and *unless.*

Introduce the Strategy

Invite pairs of students to act out the following scenarios:

• I ate a whole bag of candy.

• Rain began falling as I walked to school.

• I practiced the piano for an hour each day before the recital.

• I forgot to bring my science fair project to school.

• My best friend invited me to a birthday party.

• I didn't water the flowers for a whole week.

• My pencil lead broke during a test.

• A large dog began chasing me up a hill.

• My little brother needed help with his homework just as I was leaving to play ball.

After each performance, ask the class to determine what situation made or *caused* another event to happen and what event was the result or *effect* of that situation. Encourage students to express the relationships in complete sentences using cause-and-effect cue words, such as: Rain began to fall as I walked to school, so I held my backpack over my head and ran the rest of the way.

Model

Read "Stepping Stones" on page 106 aloud. Then model how to complete the accompanying graphic organizer (page 107) and use it to summarize the reading selection.

Practice

Have students use a copy of the blank graphic organizer on page 108 to analyze cause-and-effect relationships in other nonfiction texts, assisting as needed.

Extend and Assess

Have students complete the related writing assignment on page 109 and one or more of the extension activities on page 110. Finally, monitor their acquisition of cause and effect by using the page 110 assessment.

Use the Graphic Organizer:

Before Reading

✔ During Reading

✔ After Reading

Stepping Stones

A stitch in time saves nine. A penny saved is a penny earned. Early to bed, and early to rise, makes a man healthy, wealthy, and wise. Have you ever heard these sayings? They were written long ago by Benjamin Franklin, who was considered by many to be quite a wise man himself. How did he get that way? He learned from his experiences!

In Franklin's autobiography, he tells about a time he and his friends were catching minnows at a salt marsh around the edge of a pond. Because their feet were getting wet, Ben decided they needed some stepping stones— and he knew just where to get them.

Workers building a house nearby had piles of stones ready to use during the construction. When the men went home for the day, Ben and his friends carried the stones to the pond and built a path out to the minnows. The next morning, the workers were surprised to see their supplies missing. When they searched the area, they found the stones in the pond.

Ben and his friends were corrected by their parents. When Ben pleaded that he needed the stones, his father replied, "Nothing is useful which is not honest." From then on, Ben tried to be trustworthy in all his dealings.

Reading Selection Title _Stepping Stones_

Mark the following cue words and phrases you find in the reading selection. Then record causes and effects.

X because   ___ due to   **X** when   ___ effect

___ so   ___ consequently   ___ caused   ___ in order to

___ therefore   ___ if / then   ___ which led to   ___ unless

___ subsequently   ___ as a result   ___ resulting from

Cause: The boys' feet got wet at the salt marsh.

Effects: Ben decided to get some stepping stones. He took the stones from some workers building a house nearby. He got into trouble.

Cause: Ben argued that he and his friends needed the stones.

Effects: His father explained that something obtained dishonestly is not useful. Ben decided to try to be honest from that time on.

Now use your graphic organizer to summarize the reading selection to a partner.

Name _____ **Date** _____

Reading Selection Title _____

Mark the following cue words and phrases you find in the reading selection. Then record causes and effects.

____ because	____ due to	____ when	____ effect
____ so	____ consequently	____ caused	____ in order to
____ therefore	____ if / then	____ which led to	____ unless
____ subsequently	____ as a result	____ resulting from	

Cause:

Effects:

Cause:

Effects:

Now use your graphic organizer to summarize the reading selection to a partner.

Name _____   **Date** _____

Use the graphic organizer to record a cause-and-effect relationship you've studied in math, science, or social studies. Then write a paragraph about it using at least two of the suggested cue words or phrases.

_____

_____

_____

_____

_____

_____

_____

_____

_____

_____

_____

_____

_____

_____

Sample Topics:

Math: how a numeral changes when you move its decimal point

Science: what happens when you mix two primary colors

Social Studies: why a particular group of people immigrated to America

Extension Activities

Have students:

- read about some of Benjamin Franklin's science experiments and identify the cause-and-effect relationships that occur.

- cut out newspaper or magazine articles and highlight the cause-and-effect cue words and phrases.

- locate and share cause-and-effect relationships from their content-area textbooks.

- record cause-and-effect relationships that occur in their favorite games.

- draw a wordless series of cartoons that depict cause and effect.

- write about cause-and-effect relationships they've observed in nature.

Strategy Assessment

As students sketch their own cause-and-effect graphic organizers on notebook paper (minus the cue list), write the following statements on the board. Have students analyze them, paying special attention to cue words and phrases, and record the causes and effects on their graphic organizers.

- Benjamin Franklin was fascinated by electricity. As a result, he invented the lightning rod.

- Franklin's magazine *Poor Richard's Almanac* was a big hit because he was such a witty man.

- Franklin believed reading materials should be available to everyone, so he sold books and established a lending library.

Conduct one-on-one or small-group conferences to review students' graphic organizers, clarify any confusion, and answer any questions they still have about the strategy. Use this information to plan additional instruction, if needed, along with opportunities for periodic review and practice.

Analyzing Problem and Solution

Most readers can readily identify problems and solutions in fiction selections. A character faces a challenge and then tries to do something about it. However, problem and solution is also a common text structure in nonfiction reading. Social studies, math, and science are full of problems that people have solved through history and problems we have yet to solve. Often these problems revolve around things we want to do, information we want to find out, or situations we want to change. We're happy when we reach a turning point—the stage where the problem ends and the solution begins. Identifying real-life problems and solutions helps us understand why people and animals do the things they do, how events fit together, and how to identify the important from the unimportant as we read.

Introduce the Strategy

In small groups, have students brainstorm situations in which they or someone else had to solve a real-life problem. Then have them choose one situation to share with the class by answering the following questions: *Who had the problem? What was it? What actions were taken to solve the problem? What happened to make the solution more clear? When did things start to change? How were things different when the problem was solved? Did the solution cause any new problems? If so, what were they?*

Model

Read "Tax Troubles" on page 112 aloud. Then model how to complete the accompanying graphic organizer (page 113) and use it to summarize the reading selection.

Practice

Have students use a copy of the blank graphic organizer on page 114 to analyze problem and solution in other nonfiction texts, assisting as needed.

Extend and Assess

Have students complete the related writing assignment on page 115 and one or more of the extension activities on page 116. Finally, monitor their acquisition of problem and solution analysis by using the page 116 assessment.

Use the Graphic Organizer:

Before Reading
✔ During Reading
✔ After Reading

Tax Troubles

The colonists living in America in the mid-1700s faced many challenges. For instance, England began taxing them. The first tax law was called the Sugar Act. People had to pay an extra charge for goods like sugar and coffee coming from England. As a result, the Boston merchants refused to sell England's products. The English were forced to do away with the law.

Next, England passed the Stamp Act. This law required people to stamp all newspapers, cards, college diplomas, and other documents with a British symbol. England, of course, collected a fee for each stamp. This time the people of Boston reacted by attacking the homes of British officials and forcing them out of town. Once again, the lawmakers repealed the tax.

Soon, England passed the Townshend Act. This law placed a tax on products such as tea, lead, glass, and pigments for paint. Boston residents reacted with protests. Some protests were violent. This time England sent soldiers to enforce the act.

While patrolling the streets of Boston, the soldiers often faced angry crowds. One night in March of 1770, someone hit a soldier with a rock. The soldier fired his gun, and then the other soldiers fired. In the end, five men died and many were wounded. The soldiers were arrested, tried, acquitted, and sent back to England. However, the Townshend Act still stood, and the colonists had no choice but to pay the taxes on the items they needed.

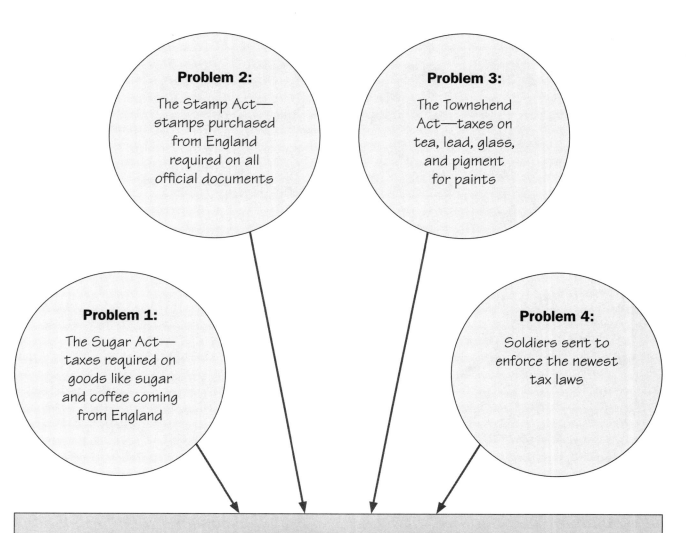

Reading Selection Title ___Tax Troubles___

As you read, record the problems mentioned in the reading selection. After you are finished, record the solutions, both successful and unsuccessful.

Problem 2:
The Stamp Act—stamps purchased from England required on all official documents

Problem 3:
The Townshend Act—taxes on tea, lead, glass, and pigment for paints

Problem 1:
The Sugar Act—taxes required on goods like sugar and coffee coming from England

Problem 4:
Soldiers sent to enforce the newest tax laws

Solutions / Attempted Solutions

1. Colonists refused to buy or sell these goods and the tax was repealed.

2. Colonists attacked the officials' homes and ran them out of town.

3. Colonists protested the tax.

4. Violence resulted in injuries and death. The soldiers were sent back to England, but the colonists still had to pay the taxes.

Now use your graphic organizer to summarize the reading selection to a partner.

Name _____ **Date** _____

Reading Selection Title _____

As you read, record the problems mentioned in the reading selection. After you are finished, record the solutions, both successful and unsuccessful.

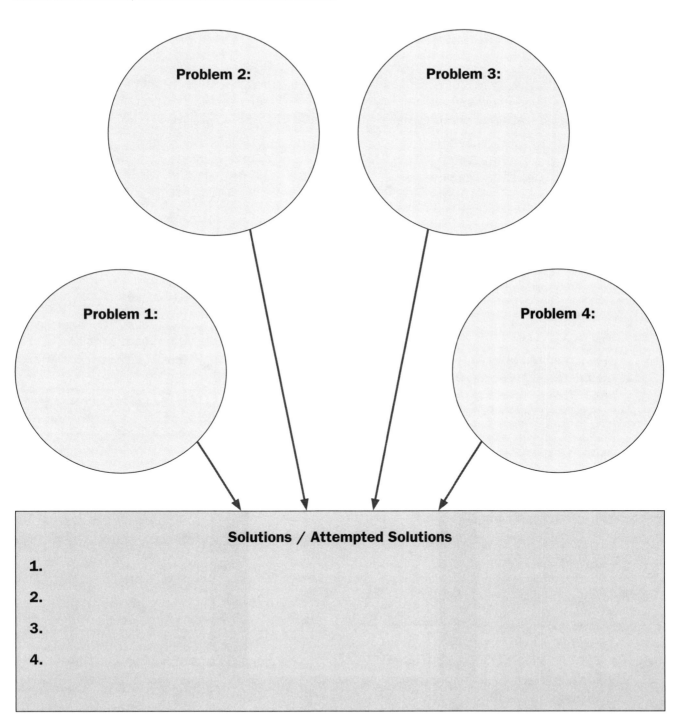

Now use your graphic organizer to summarize the reading selection to a partner.

Name _____   **Date** _____

Use the graphic organizer to record a problem and solution you've studied in math, science, or social studies. Then write a paragraph about it.

_____

_____

_____

_____

_____

_____

_____

_____

_____

_____

_____

_____

_____

_____

_____

Sample Topics:

Math: converting measurements from the standard system to the metric system

Science: reducing lunchroom waste

Social Studies: recovering from a weather-related natural disaster

Extension Activities

Have students:

- use the graphic organizer to record problems and solutions in another article about U.S. history.

- cut out newspaper articles in which the heading indicates a problem and the text presents a solution.

- locate and share problems and solutions from their content-area textbooks.

- write advice columns for problems encountered in nonfiction reading.

- conduct a "talk show" in which one student interviews another about a real-world problem and the "guest expert" explains what is being done to solve it.

- use the graphic organizer to record problems and solutions in a documentary viewed in class or at home.

Strategy Assessment

Have students sketch their own problem/solution graphic organizers on notebook paper. Locate a brief, interesting article that includes a real-world problem and solution. Read it aloud slowly, pausing periodically so students can record information on their graphic organizers. If needed, read it once more at a quicker pace so students can check their work.

Conduct one-on-one or small-group conferences to review students' graphic organizers, clarify any confusion, and answer any questions they still have about the strategy. Use this information to plan additional instruction, if needed, along with opportunities for periodic review and practice.

Identifying Fact and Opinion

A fact is a statement that can be proven. An opinion, on the other hand, represents a subjective belief or feeling. Readers generally accept facts, but they can agree or disagree with opinions. However, deciding whether a statement is a fact or an opinion can sometimes be difficult. In addition, a reader who agrees with an opinion might consider it a fact. To avoid misinterpretations, readers need to carefully evaluate the text and determine the author's purpose and point of view in making a particular statement. Sometimes the authors provide cue words and phrases such as *think, feel, maybe,* or *assume* to identify opinions and *actual, recognized, based on,* or *proven* to identify facts. Other times, readers have to "read between the lines." Either way, careful readers are wary of exaggerations and all-or-nothing words such as *always, everyone, never,* and *no one.* In short—critical judgment is required.

Introduce the Strategy

Before beginning, prepare and photocopy a list of ten or more statements that are a mixture of facts and opinions. Have students work in pairs to label which is which. Remind them to ask themselves: *Can the statement be proven? Can I think of an example when the statement might not be true?* When everyone is finished, have each partnership share one or two results and defend their answers.

Model

Read "Monster Mania" on page 118 aloud. Then model how to complete the accompanying graphic organizer (page 119) and use it to summarize the reading selection.

Practice

Have students use a copy of the blank graphic organizer on page 120 to identify facts and opinions in other nonfiction texts, assisting as needed.

Extend and Assess

Have students complete the related writing assignment on page 121 and one or more of the extension activities on page 122. Finally, monitor their acquisition of fact and opinion identification by using the page 122 assessment.

Use the Graphic Organizer:

Before Reading

✔ During Reading

✔ After Reading

Monster Mania

History is full of monster tales. Reported sightings of strange creatures turn up in cultures around the world. As these mysterious stories are told and retold, details can become fuzzy.

One popular example is The Monster of Loch Ness. A man in Scotland thought he saw a creature in the water. Villagers who passed on his story made the beast increasingly large and frightening. Soon a reporter decided to print the story in a newspaper. The editor called the creature a monster, and the legend was born.

Another well-known monster is Big Foot, said to live in the western United States. Like descriptions of the Loch Ness Monster, the stories about Big Foot vary from one person to the next. Some say he's as big as a man. Others say he's nearly seven feet tall. Some tell of a frightening creature covered in hair with sharp teeth and bear claws. Others describe Big Foot with more human-like traits. No one seems to agree on much about him except his status as a monster.

The decision to accept or not accept these claims falls on the listener. What should we believe? *The Random House Unabridged Dictionary* says a monster is *a legendary animal*. However, other definitions say a monster is *any creature so ugly as to frighten people* or *any animal or thing huge in size*. Depending on which meaning you choose, a monster could be made up or real. What do you think?

Reading Selection Title ___Monster Mania___

Mark the following cue words or phrases you find in the reading selection. Then record facts and opinions.

X think/thought	___ possibly	___ imagine	___ actual	___ researched
___ feel	**X** said to	___ dream of	___ sure	___ recognized
___ may	___ sense	___ picture	___ definite	___ known
___ maybe	___ suppose	**X** believe	___ unquestionable	___ based on
X could be	___ assume	___ positive	___ exact	___ without a doubt
___ perhaps	___ guess	___ certain	___ proof	

Facts:
"History is full of monster tales."
"Reported sightings of strange creatures turn up in cultures around the world."
"Soon a reporter decided to print the story in a newspaper."
"The editor called the creature a monster."
"The decision to accept or not accept these claims falls on the listener."
"The Random House Unabridged Dictionary says . . . "

Opinions:	**Whose Opinion?**
Details become fuzzy.	author's
Loch Ness is popular.	author's
A monster lives in the water in Loch Ness.	many people's
The monster is large and frightening.	many people's
An editor is responsible for the Loch Ness legend.	author's
Big Foot is well known.	author's
Big Foot lives in the western United States.	many people's
Big Foot looks big/normal-sized/hairy/human-like, etc.	many people's
Monsters could be made up or real.	author's

Now use your graphic organizer to summarize the reading selection to a partner.

Name _____   **Date** _____

Reading Selection Title _____

Mark the following cue words or phrases you find in the reading selection. Then record facts and opinions.

___ think/thought	___ possibly	___ imagine	___ actual	___ researched
___ feel	___ said to	___ dream of	___ sure	___ recognized
___ may	___ sense	___ picture	___ definite	___ known
___ maybe	___ suppose	___ believe	___ unquestionable	___ based on
___ could be	___ assume	___ positive	___ exact	___ without a doubt
___ perhaps	___ guess	___ certain	___ proof	

Facts:

Opinions:	**Whose Opinion?**

Now use your graphic organizer to summarize the reading selection to a partner.

Name _____ **Date** _____

Use the graphic organizer to record facts and opinions about a topic you've studied in math, science, or social studies. Then write a paragraph about it using at least two of the suggested cue words and phrases.

_____

_____

_____

_____

_____

_____

_____

_____

_____

_____

_____

_____

_____

Sample Topics:

Math: daylight savings time

Science: archeological digs

Social Studies: political ads in newspapers

Extension Activities

Have students:

- use the graphic organizer to record facts and opinions in an article specifically about the Loch Ness Monster or Big Foot.

- cut out newspaper or magazine articles and highlight any fact or opinion cue words and phrases.

- locate and share facts and opinions from their content-area textbooks.

- pretend an alien spacecraft just landed and describe the aliens using both facts and opinions.

- write general topics on slips of paper, such as *sports, music, chores, shopping, reading, friends, drawing,* or *weather* and then take turns drawing out a topic and stating three facts and three opinions about it.

- use the graphic organizer to record facts and opinions stated in a content-area video viewed in class.

Strategy Assessment

As students sketch their own fact/opinion graphic organizers on notebook paper (minus the cue list), write the following statements on the board. Have students analyze them, paying special attention to cue words and phrases, and record the results on their graphic organizers.

- I think everyone in the class will be grouchy if we have to write book reports over the weekend.

- Perhaps two yards of fabric will be enough to make curtains for my bedroom.

- The buffalo is recognized as the state animal in Kansas.

- Based on ticket sales, this was our most popular school play ever.

- Yellow could be a nice color for the bulletin board background.

- The actual date of the field trip is a week from Thursday.

Conduct one-on-one or small-group conferences to review students' graphic organizers, clarify any confusion, and answer any questions they still have about the strategy. Use this information to plan additional instruction, if needed, along with opportunities for periodic review and practice.

Identifying Persuasive Techniques

Mom, may I have some friends over on Saturday? I don't see anything on the calendar that would interfere. I can do all my chores Friday after school. Plus, we can all talk about our science fair project while we're hanging out." Wow—this student understands persuasion! We employ persuasion when we try to convince someone to agree with our ideas or point of view. We state a request or an opinion and support it with carefully selected reasons, facts, and details. In persuasive writing, authors use additional techniques, such as choosing catchy titles, explaining why the opposite opinion is not a good choice, or issuing a "call to action."

Introduce the Strategy

Collect and display several print advertisements, particularly those aimed at children and teenagers. Have students highlight words that express the main purpose of each advertisement and underline reasons, facts, and details that support the advertisers' opinions. Next, have students decide whether the advertisement is (1) trying to get them to take action, such as attending an event or purchasing a product, or (2) warning them away from an unwise decision or unhealthy habit. Use these categories to create two classroom collages: *Persuading For* and *Persuading Against*. Invite students to bring in their own ads to add to the collages.

Model

Read "Going to the Dogs . . . and Cats" on page 124 aloud. Then model how to complete the accompanying graphic organizer (page 125) and use it to summarize the reading selection.

Practice

Have students use a copy of the blank graphic organizer on page 126 to identify persuasive techniques in other nonfiction texts, assisting as needed.

Extend and Assess

Have students complete the related writing assignment on page 127 and one or more of the extension activities on page 128. Finally, monitor their acquisition of persuasive technique identification by using the page 128 assessment.

Use the Graphic Organizer:

✔ Before Reading

✔ During Reading

✔ After Reading

Going to the Dogs . . . and Cats

Did you know the United States is home to millions of stray cats and dogs? This fact is sad, but true. Sometimes people can no longer take care of their pets or no longer wish to do so. They abandon them, assuming that someone else will find and take care of the animals. However, things don't always work out that way.

Sometimes strays give birth to more strays, and the population grows. The lucky ones get rescued by new owners. Others live a rough life, daily searching for food, water, and shelter. Stray dogs and cats can spread disease and harm other animals and people. Cats, in particular, kill wildlife like birds and small mammals.

You can help cut down the number of stray and abandoned animals. If you are looking for a new pet, make certain to get one you can keep for a long time. Remember that dogs can live more than twelve years, and cats can live to be twenty. Once you've made your decision, go to a shelter and adopt a pet. Shelters have cats and dogs in all sizes, colors, and breeds.

Next, make sure to get your new pet spayed or neutered so it cannot produce offspring. Get a collar and tag or ID for your pet to prevent loss. Most of all, love your pet, treat it well, and keep it safe. Your pet will love you back, which will more than reward you for your efforts.

Remember the two ways to prevent and help strays: (1) Adopt a pet from a shelter. (2) Never desert a pet. If everyone follows these suggestions, our country will be a happier place for dogs and cats.

Reading Selection Title _Going to the Dogs . . . and Cats_

Select the persuasive techniques the author uses and record evidence.

The author . . .	Yes or No?	Evidence
chooses a title that catches my attention	Yes	"Going to the dogs" is an old saying—it has a double meaning here.
clearly states an opinion	Yes	We need to cut down the number of stray and abandoned animals.
states more than one reason for his/her opinion	Yes	(1) strays create more strays (2) many strays live a rough life (3) strays can spread disease and cause harm
arranges facts and details in a logical order, such as least important to most important	Yes	least serious to most serious
states why the opposite opinion is not a good choice	Yes	(see reasons above)
anticipates and addresses possible questions or objections	Yes	When choosing a pet, consider how long it might live.
chooses words that are convincing	Yes	(1) sad, but true (2) the lucky ones (3) a rough life (4) disease and harm (5) you can help (6) more than reward you (7) happier place
avoids words that are pushy, rude, or overly emotional or negative	Yes	(1) uses "sad"—not "horrible" (2) uses "make sure"—not "must" or "have to"
uses a tone that matches the topic—humorous or serious	Yes	serious
uses cue words such as *should, must, never, always, everyone, be sure, remember*	Yes	make certain, make sure, remember, never, everyone
includes a command or "call to action"	Yes	Adopt from a shelter and never desert a pet.
sounds convincing	Yes	appeals to both logic and feelings

Now use your graphic organizer to summarize the reading selection to a partner.

Name _____ **Date** _____

Reading Selection Title _____

Select the persuasive techniques the author uses and record evidence.

The author . . .	Yes or No?	Evidence
chooses a title that catches my attention		
clearly states an opinion		
states more than one reason for his/her opinion		
arranges facts and details in a logical order, such as least important to most important		
states why the opposite opinion is not a good choice		
anticipates and addresses possible questions or objections		
chooses words that are convincing		
avoids words that are pushy, rude, or overly emotional or negative		
uses a tone that matches the topic—humorous or serious		
uses cue words such as *should, must, never, always, everyone, be sure, remember*		
includes a command or "call to action"		
sounds convincing		

Now use your graphic organizer to summarize the reading selection to a partner.

Name _____   Date _____

Use the graphic organizer to record persuasive techniques related to math, science, or social studies. Then write a paragraph about it.

_____

_____

_____

_____

_____

_____

_____

_____

_____

_____

_____

_____

_____

_____

_____

Sample Topics:

Math: why we need to learn basic math facts when calculators are readily available

Science: how a school science fair could benefit students

Social Studies: why we should learn about customary greetings in other countries

Extension Activities

Have students:

- review the advertisements used in the "Introduce the Strategy" activity and then write and illustrate their own ads for or against a particular product or activity.

- read some editorials in the newspaper and underline persuasive words such as *should, must, never, always, everyone, be sure, to,* or *remember.*

- locate and share examples of persuasive techniques from their content-area textbooks.

- locate and share examples of poems that humorously try to persuade the reader to do or not do something, such as those by Shel Silverstein or Jack Prelutsky.

- work with partners to put on skits that involve persuasive techniques.

- use the graphic organizer to analyze a famous speech, such as "The Gettysburg Address," and then write their own persuasive speeches to present to the class.

Strategy Assessment

The set-up for this assessment departs from the usual procedure employed in *Show Me!* Because the strategy requires a detailed checklist, students should not be required to sketch the graphic organizer on their own. Instead, supply photocopies of page 126 for each student. Locate a brief persuasive article, editorial, advertisement, or letter, such as a brochure from The American Society for the Prevention of Cruelty to Animals. Read it aloud slowly, pausing periodically so students can record information on their graphic organizers. If needed, read it once more at a quicker pace so students can check their work.

Conduct one-on-one or small-group conferences to review students' graphic organizers, clarify any confusion, and answer any questions they still have about the strategy. Use this information to plan additional instruction, if needed, along with opportunities for periodic review and practice.

Comparing and Contrasting Information and Ideas

Comparing is finding similarities. Contrasting is finding differences. In nonfiction, effective readers look for ways information and ideas are alike and different in order to better understand them. Often, an author's text organization includes direct comparisons and contrasts using cue words such as *like, also, however,* or *but.* Other times the similarities and differences are not openly stated and left to the reader to figure out. Either way, actively comparing and contrasting helps us gain additional insight into a text and form opinions about the topic.

Introduce the Strategy

One at a time, call out a series of descriptive phrases that likely apply to some members of your class, such as *has a pet, oldest child in the family, likes spaghetti, enjoys roller-skating,* and *made your bed this morning.* Ask students who fit that category to stand and others to remain seated. Explain that discovering ways classmates are alike is called *comparing* and discovering ways they are different is called *contrasting.* Then invite volunteers to create oral sentences about what they observed as you record any compare/contrast cue words they use on the board. For example: *Mario made his bed this morning,* but *I didn't. Jessie and I like the* same *food—spaghetti.* Even though *I enjoy roller-skating, Kim doesn't. Paul and I* both *have pets and we're the oldest kids in our families,* too.

Model

Read "Rain Forests" on page 130 aloud. Then model how to complete the accompanying graphic organizer (page 131) and use it to summarize the reading selection.

Practice

Have students use a copy of the blank graphic organizer on page 132 to compare and contrast information and ideas in other nonfiction texts, assisting as needed.

Extend and Assess

Have students complete the related writing assignment on page 133 and one or more of the extension activities on page 134. Finally, monitor their acquisition of comparing and contrasting by using the page 134 assessment.

Use the Graphic Organizer:

Before Reading

✔ During Reading

✔ After Reading

Rain Forests

You've likely heard of the Amazon Rain Forest in South America. It's a tropical forest. Did you know the United States has a rain forest, too? It's in the Olympic Mountains of Washington. It's called a temperate forest. The weather can be warm or cold, while a tropical forest is always warm.

The temperate forest gets about seventeen inches of rain each year. Unlike tropical areas, temperate forest animals include bears, elk, and slugs as big as your foot. In the canopy, you'll see owls and flying squirrels. No people live in this forest.

Tropical forests get much more rain —about thirty-five inches of rain in a year. Colorful macaws call to one another. Poisonous frogs live among the trees and plants. In the canopy, you'll find sloths and flying monkeys. Native tribes have lived in the Amazon forests for thousands of years.

All rain forests face dangers. One is pollution from large cities nearby. In addition, lumber companies want the wood from rainforest trees. We must all be aware of the threats rain forests have in common and work to protect our forests all over the world.

Reading Selection Title   Rain Forests

Mark the following cue words or phrases you find in the reading selection. Then record things that are alike and things that are different about two subjects.

X too	___ like	___ however	___ unless	___ otherwise
X both	___ also	___ but	**X** while	___ either
___ alike	___ similar	___ yet	___ different	___ on the contrary
___ likewise	**X** in addition	___ on the other hand	**X** unlike	___ even though
___ same	___ as well as	___ although	___ in contrast	___ instead
X all	**X** in common	**X** more/less	___ not only	

Things That Are Different	
Subject 1: Temperate Rain Forest	**Subject 2:** Tropical Rain Forest
sometimes cold	always warm
17" of rain per year	35" of rain per year
bears	poisonous frogs
elk	sloths
owls	macaws
flying squirrels	flying monkeys
no people	people

Things That Are the Same

have many plants and animals

in danger from pollution

in danger from lumber companies

need our protection

Now use your graphic organizer to summarize the reading selection to a partner.

Name _____ **Date** _____

Reading Selection Title _____

Mark the following cue words or phrases you find in the reading selection. Then record things that are alike and things that are different about two subjects.

___ too	___ like	___ however	___ unless	___ otherwise
___ both	___ also	___ but	___ while	___ either
___ alike	___ similar	___ yet	___ different	___ on the contrary
___ likewise	___ in addition	___ on the other hand	___ unlike	___ even though
___ same	___ as well as	___ although	___ in contrast	___ instead
___ all	___ in common	___ more/less	___ not only	

Things That Are Different	
Subject 1:	**Subject 2:**

Things That Are the Same

Now use your graphic organizer to summarize the reading selection to a partner.

Name _____ **Date** _____

Use the graphic organizer to compare and contrast two topics or ideas you've studied in math, science, or social studies. Then write a paragraph about them using at least two of the suggested cue words or phrases.

_____

_____

_____

_____

_____

_____

_____

_____

_____

_____

_____

_____

_____

_____

Sample Topics:

Math: multiplication and division

Science: freshwater fish and ocean fish

Social Studies: your state and another state

Extension Activities

Have students:

- compare and contrast two other habitats, such as the Mojave Desert in the United States and the Sahara Desert in Africa.

- cut out newspaper or magazine articles and highlight any compare/contrast cue words and phrases.

- locate and share examples of comparing and contrasting from their content-area textbooks.

- compare and contrast two favorite sports.

- compare and contrast a movie with its sequel.

- follow the same craft directions with a partner and then compare and contrast the resulting creations.

Strategy Assessment

As students sketch their own compare/contrast graphic organizers on notebook paper (minus the cue list), write the following statements on the board. Have students analyze them, paying special attention to cue words and phrases, and record the results on their graphic organizers.

- All grasslands occur in hot, dry climates.

- Grasslands in the United States are called *prairies*. However, they're called *savannas* in Africa.

- Prairie dogs and mule deer live in prairies, while giraffes, zebras, and lions live in savannas.

Conduct one-on-one or small-group conferences to review students' graphic organizers, clarify any confusion, and answer any questions they still have about the strategy. Use this information to plan additional instruction, if needed, along with opportunities for periodic review and practice.

Sequencing Events— Time Order in History

Nonfiction authors often describe historical events in the order in which they occurred. Sometimes they use cue words and phrases such as *then, in 1800, before,* or *finally.* Other times the reader must use logic to recognize time order relationships. By paying close attention to the sequence of events, readers can picture what happened in the past, see how the events fit together, and better understand and remember text details.

Introduce the Strategy

Have students create personal time lines on drawing paper. Say: *At the top of the paper, draw a circle or square. Fill it in with your full name and date of birth. Then draw more circles or squares at equal intervals on your paper, one for each year of your life. Try to fill in each one with an important event. For example, you learned to walk somewhere around age one. What else have you learned to do? Did you go to preschool? Has your family moved? Have you started a hobby, taken lessons, played a sport, or adopted a pet?* Invite students to illustrate their time lines, and allow time for them to share them with the class. Display in the classroom.

Model

Read "Muscle Cars of the 1960s" on page 136 aloud. Then model how to complete the accompanying graphic organizer (page 137) and use it to summarize the reading selection.

Practice

Have students use a copy of the blank graphic organizer on page 138 to sequence events in other nonfiction texts, assisting as needed.

Extend and Assess

Have students complete the related writing assignment on page 139 and one or more of the extension activities on page 140. Finally, monitor their acquisition of time order by using the page 140 assessment.

Use the Graphic Organizer:

Before Reading

✔ During Reading

✔ After Reading

Muscle Cars of the 1960s

What's your dream vehicle? Some people wish for a modern car like the 2004 Subaru WRX. Others dream of a classic car like a 1965 Ford Mustang with its 289 V8 engine. It wasn't the only fast car in 1965, either. Ned Jarrett won the NASCAR finals in a Ford Galaxie.

Cars like these were known as *super cars*. Most were mid-sized. However, small cars like the Mustang were also called *pony cars*. Then, in the 1970s, people renamed them *muscle cars*. All had large V8 engines and were priced to sell.

The next muscle car came out in 1966. The Dodge Charger fastback sported a 318 motor. Buyers who wanted more power could get a 383 V8 or even a 426 Hemi. This began a new era for Dodge.

A muscle car still in demand today is the 1967 Pontiac GTO. It has a 400 V8 engine. Fans know the GTO by the sound it makes coming down the street. Chevy came out with the Corvette 427 in 1968 and the Camaro 427 in 1969. Both remain popular.

Modern or classic? New or old? Whatever your dream car may be, these muscle cars will always remain on someone's list!

Reading Selection Title ___Muscle Cars of the 1960s___

Mark the following cue words and phrases you find in the reading selection. Then record events or details in time order.

___ first	___ after	___ while	___ before	___ at the same time
___ second	___ tomorrow	___ yesterday	___ soon	**X** always
___ third	___ later	___ meanwhile	___ last	___ during
X next	___ finally	___ as	**X** still	**X** today
X then	___ now	**X** in/on (day or date)	**X** began	___ when

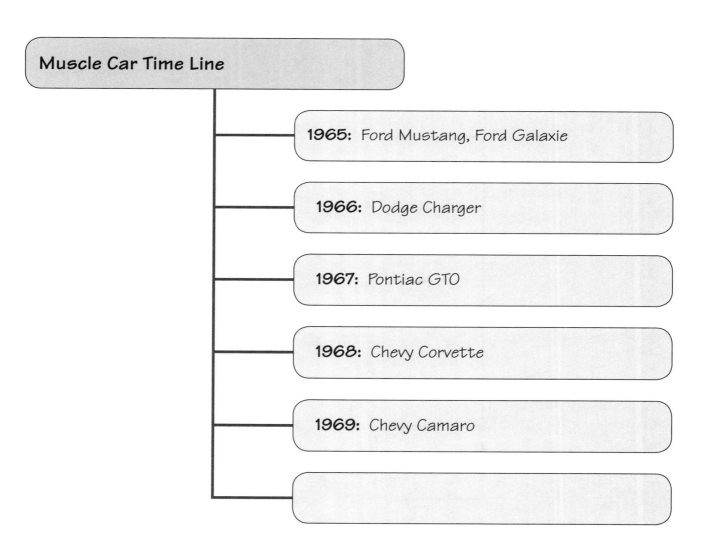

Muscle Car Time Line

1965: Ford Mustang, Ford Galaxie

1966: Dodge Charger

1967: Pontiac GTO

1968: Chevy Corvette

1969: Chevy Camaro

Now use your graphic organizer to summarize the reading selection to a partner.

Name _____   **Date** _____

Reading Selection Title _____

Mark the following cue words and phrases you find in the reading selection. Then record events or details in time order.

___ first	___ after	___ while	___ before	___ at the same time
___ second	___ tomorrow	___ yesterday	___ soon	___ always
___ third	___ later	___ meanwhile	___ last	___ during
___ next	___ finally	___ as	___ still	___ today
___ then	___ now	___ in/on (day or date)	___ began	___ when

Now use your graphic organizer to summarize the reading selection to a partner.

Name _____ **Date** _____

Use the graphic organizer to record a time order sequence you've studied in math, science, or social studies. Then write a paragraph about it using at least two of the suggested cue words or phrases.

_____

_____

_____

_____

_____

_____

_____

_____

_____

_____

_____

_____

_____

_____

Sample Topics:

Math: computers then and now
Science: inventions in the 1900s
Social Studies: the Gold Rush

Extension Activities

Have students:

- use the graphic organizer to sequence events in another article about sports cars.

- cut out newspaper or magazine articles that describe past events and highlight any sequencing words and phrases.

- locate and share time-ordered events from their content-area textbooks.

- use the graphic organizer to sequence events while viewing a documentary.

- draw a series of pictures or cartoons that depict historical events, scramble them, and have classmates try to sequence them in the correct order.

- use the graphic organizer to sequence an event that occurs in nature, such as a caterpillar changing into a butterfly.

Strategy Assessment

Have students sketch their own sequencing graphic organizers on notebook paper (minus the cue list). Locate a brief, interesting article that describes a past event. Read it aloud slowly, pausing periodically so students can record information on their graphic organizers. Remind them to listen for cue words and phrases as well. If needed, read it once more at a quicker pace so students can check their work.

Conduct one-on-one or small-group conferences to review students' graphic organizers, clarify any confusion, and answer any questions they still have about the strategy. Use this information to plan additional instruction, if needed, along with opportunities for periodic review and practice.

Sequencing Events— Following Directions

Following directions is an essential skill used in all aspects of life, from repairing a bicycle to preparing a feast to writing a limerick. In how-to texts, authors describe activities that need to occur in a particular order using cue words and phrases such as *first, then, after, when,* or *before.* By paying attention to the sequence of events, the reader can picture what the author explains, carry out the steps in proper order, and better understand the process involved.

Introduce the Strategy

Have students tell you the steps needed to complete a simple classroom task, such as cleaning out a desk, while you record their ideas on the chalkboard. When they're done, begin carrying out the steps. Have fun with your demonstration by following the directions quite literally. For example, if the first step is to put everything on top of the desk, begin piling on items from all over the room, not from inside the messy desk. Once you've completed (or are unable to complete) the task, have students suggest details that will make their instructions more clear.

Model

Read "Fly a Paper Airplane" on page 142 aloud. Then model how to complete the accompanying graphic organizer (page 143) and use it to summarize the reading selection.

Practice

Have students use a copy of the blank graphic organizer on page 144 to sequence direction events in other nonfiction texts, assisting as needed.

Extend and Assess

Have students complete the related writing assignment on page 145 and one or more of the extension activities on page 146. Finally, monitor their acquisition of sequencing by using the page 146 assessment.

Use the Graphic Organizer:

Before Reading

✔ During Reading

After Reading

Fly a Paper Airplane

Picture this! Your sister is sitting at the kitchen table doing homework and humming along to the radio. Suddenly— ZING! Your paper airplane flies past her shoulder. You both laugh. She picks up the airplane and studies it closely. "How did you do that?" she asks. Here's what you tell her:

First, find a thin, white paper plate. Color or decorate the bottom of the plate. Next, find a large paper clip and a piece of tape.

Begin by folding the plate in half with the white side in. Then open it up again. Turn the plate until the fold line is straight up and down, like clock hands at 6:00.

Continuing to picture a clock face, bend down the upper left section of the plate between the 9 and the 12. Then bend down the upper right section of the plate between the 12 and the 3. These will overlap a bit. After that, redo the original center fold.

Now bend one of the top folded edges out and down to the center fold to make a wing. Turn the plate over and make the same bend on the other side. Tape across the top where the two wings touch. To finish, fasten the paper clip to the plane's pointed nose. Finally, give your plane a throw, nose first. ZING!

After your sister has tested her plane, challenge her to a fly-off. The plane that flies the farthest is the winner!

Reading Selection Title _Fly a Paper Airplane_

Mark the following cue words or phrases you find in the reading selection. Then record the directions in order.

X first	**X** after	**X** now	___ before	___ always
___ second	___ when	___ while	___ last	___ as
___ third	**X** finish	___ during	___ still	**X** until
X next	___ later	___ meanwhile	___ at the same time	
X then	**X** finally	**X** continue	**X** begin	

Task: _Making a paper airplane_

Decorate a thin, white paper plate.

↓

Fold the plate in half.

↓

Open the plate back up with the fold line straight up and down.

↓

Bend in the upper left and upper right sections of the plate.

↓

Fold the plate in half again.

↓

Bend the top folded edges out and down to the center fold.

↓

Tape across the top where the wings touch.

↓

Paperclip the nose and fly your plane.

Now use your graphic organizer to summarize the reading selection to a partner.

Name _____ **Date** _____

Reading Selection Title _____

Mark the following cue words or phrases you find in the reading selection. Then record the directions in order.

___ first	___ after	___ now	___ before	___ always
___ second	___ when	___ while	___ last	___ as
___ third	___ finish	___ during	___ still	___ until
___ next	___ later	___ meanwhile	___ at the same time	
___ then	___ finally	___ continue	___ begin	

Task: _____

```
┌─────────────────────────────────────────────────┐
│                                                   │
└─────────────────────────────────────────────────┘
                         ↓
┌─────────────────────────────────────────────────┐
│                                                   │
└─────────────────────────────────────────────────┘
                         ↓
┌─────────────────────────────────────────────────┐
│                                                   │
└─────────────────────────────────────────────────┘
                         ↓
┌─────────────────────────────────────────────────┐
│                                                   │
└─────────────────────────────────────────────────┘
                         ↓
┌─────────────────────────────────────────────────┐
│                                                   │
└─────────────────────────────────────────────────┘
                         ↓
┌─────────────────────────────────────────────────┐
│                                                   │
└─────────────────────────────────────────────────┘
                         ↓
┌─────────────────────────────────────────────────┐
│                                                   │
└─────────────────────────────────────────────────┘
                         ↓
┌─────────────────────────────────────────────────┐
│                                                   │
└─────────────────────────────────────────────────┘
```

Now use your graphic organizer to summarize the reading selection to a partner.

Name _____   **Date** _____

Use the graphic organizer to record directions you've learned about in math, science, or social studies. Then write a paragraph about it using at least two of the suggested cue words or phrases.

_____

_____

_____

_____

_____

_____

_____

_____

_____

_____

_____

_____

_____

Sample Topics:

Math: figuring the area of a bulletin board

Science: conducting an experiment using the scientific method

Social Studies: taking a census

Extension Activities

Have students:

- follow the directions in the reading selection and have their own fly-off.

- cut out newspaper or magazine how-to articles and highlight any sequencing cue words and phrases.

- locate and share sequenced directions from their content-area textbooks.

- use the graphic organizer to plan demonstrations to present to the class.

- rewrite a simple recipe in paragraph form using sequencing cue words and phrases.

- use the graphic organizer to explain the steps in playing a simple game.

Strategy Assessment

Have students sketch their own sequencing graphic organizers on notebook paper (minus the cue list). Locate a brief, interesting how-to article or simple recipe. Read it aloud slowly, pausing periodically so students can record information on their graphic organizers. Remind them to listen for cue words and phrases as well. If needed, read it once more at a quicker pace so students can check their work.

Conduct one-on-one or small-group conferences to review students' graphic organizers, clarify any confusion, and answer any questions they still have about the strategy. Use this information to plan additional instruction, if needed, along with opportunities for periodic review and practice.

Restating to Monitor Meaning

Restating is a process in which readers use their own words to verbalize or write about what they've read in order to demonstrate comprehension of the material. Restating requires organized thinking processes and the ability to discern important from unimportant information. Restating is a powerful tool for readers who wish to self-monitor whether or not they understand a text. To get even more out of the strategy, readers can review the selection, pick up additional details, and elaborate on their original statements.

Introduce the Strategy

Restate information from a nonfiction read-aloud you have shared with the class. Then ask students to guess the name of the book. Once they do, invite volunteers to retell information from other read-alouds or familiar nonfiction library books and have the other students guess the titles. Point out that the ability to accurately restate details shows that the reader or listener paid close attention and successfully processed the information.

Model

Read "Chinese New Year" on page 148 aloud. Then model how to complete the accompanying graphic organizer (page 149) and use it to summarize the reading selection.

Practice

Have students use a copy of the blank graphic organizer on page 150 to restate information in other nonfiction texts, assisting as needed.

Extend and Assess

Have students complete the related writing assignment on page 151 and one or more of the extension activities on page 152. Finally, monitor their acquisition of restating by using the page 152 assessment.

Use the Graphic Organizer:

Before Reading

✔ During Reading

✔ After Reading

Chinese New Year

The Chinese New Year marks the start of spring. Many traditions go into this occasion. However, it is more than just a party. The holiday is used to wish friends and family luck, health, and happiness.

The celebration begins with elaborate preparations. Families work together to clean their houses. Sweeping the dirt out the door sweeps away bad luck that may be hiding in the home and makes room for the new year's good fortune. Some families even go the cemetery to clean the tombstones of their departed family members.

Next, families hang banners of red and gold with lucky messages written on them. Then they set plants and flowers all around the house. If the buds bloom on New Year's Day, everyone in the family will have a good year. Peach and plum tree branches are used to bring long life.

Many families shop for new clothes for the new year. The clothing is often red, a symbol of happiness. They get haircuts. They add lime leaves to their bath water to make themselves extra clean. They pay off their bills, and they forgive anyone who has hurt them in the past year.

On New Year's Eve, the families seal the doors to their homes with red paper. Then they have a feast of meat, vegetables, and noodles. The table is set for every member of the family, even if some cannot be there. Some family members stay up all night to make sure everyone stays safe.

On New Year's Day, the red paper seals are broken and the doors are opened to let in the year's good luck. Everyone is on his or her best behavior, because whatever happens on this day is a sign of what the new year will bring. Children are given paper money in red envelopes. Firecrackers are set off outside. Parades with dancing dragons and parties take place all over the neighborhoods. All the people are happy in their good fortune.

Reading Selection Title _Chinese New Year_

Record the most important facts and details from each paragraph in your own words.

Paragraph # 1

> marks the start of spring
>
> many traditions
>
> more than just a party
>
> used to wish friends and family luck, health, and happiness

Paragraph # 2 & 3

> clean house; sweep out dirt and bad luck to make room for good fortune
>
> clean tombstones
>
> hang banners with lucky messages
>
> set plants & flowers around the house
>
> use peach & plum branches to bring long life

Paragraph # 4

> shop for clothes, especially red for happiness
>
> get haircuts
>
> bathe with lime leaves to get extra clean
>
> pay off bills
>
> forgive everyone

Paragraph # 5 & 6

> seal the door
> serve a feast for everyone in the family
> stay up all night to be safe
> break seals, open doors
> stay on best behavior
> give children paper money in red envelopes
> have firecrackers & parades

Now use your graphic organizer to summarize the reading selection to a partner.

Name _____ **Date** _____

Reading Selection Title _____

Record the most important facts and details from each paragraph in your own words.

Paragraph # ➡

Paragraph # ➡

Paragraph # ➡

Paragraph # ➡

Now use your graphic organizer to summarize the reading selection to a partner.

Name _____ **Date** _____

Use the graphic organizer to restate information about a topic you've studied in math, science, or social studies. Then write a paragraph about it.

_____

_____

_____

_____

_____

_____

_____

_____

_____

_____

_____

_____

_____

_____

Sample Topics:

Math: Roman numerals
Science: the Food Pyramid
Social Studies: Cinco de Mayo

Extension Activities

Have students:

- use the graphic organizer to restate information in another article about a holiday.

- cut out newspaper or magazine articles, highlight the most important points, and then restate the information in their own words.

- use the graphic organizer to restate information from their content-area textbooks.

- use the graphic organizer to restate information in a content-area video viewed in the classroom.

- draw rather than write the most important points of a self-selected article and then use the drawings to restate the article to a partner.

- use the graphic organizer to restate the most important points they hear in your current classroom read-aloud.

Strategy Assessment

Have students sketch their own restating graphic organizers on notebook paper. Locate a brief, interesting article. Read it aloud slowly, pausing periodically so students can record information on their graphic organizers. If needed, read it once more at a quicker pace so students can check their work.

Conduct one-on-one or small-group conferences to review students' graphic organizers, clarify any confusion, and answer any questions they still have about the strategy. Use this information to plan additional instruction, if needed, along with opportunities for periodic review and practice.

Making Judgments

A judgment is an opinion, belief, or preference. We use our five senses along with our prior experiences, emotions, and logic to make judgments throughout the day. When interacting with a text, we make judgments about whether the topic is interesting, whether the information is accurate, and whether we agree or disagree with the author's ideas. In addition, we often make judgments that lead us to take action or make personal choices based on what we read.

Introduce the Strategy

Ask questions involving judgments, such as: *Do you prefer cereal or eggs for breakfast? Why? Would you rather read a scary story or a book of poetry? Why? Do you think reading a newspaper or watching a television news show is a better way to keep up on current events? Why? Do you believe we might find life on other planets someday? Why or why not?* After discussing each one, ask students to make a list of four or five similar questions to ask a classmate and then report back to the class. Point out that we make judgments based on what we observe, how it makes us feel, what we have learned in the past, and what seems to make sense at the time.

Model

Read "To Play or Not to Play: The Pros and Cons of Computer Games" on page 154 aloud. Then model how to complete the accompanying graphic organizer (page 155) and use it to summarize the reading selection.

Practice

Have students use a copy of the blank graphic organizer on page 156 to make judgments in other nonfiction texts, assisting as needed.

Extend and Assess

Have students complete the related writing assignment on page 157 and one or more of the extension activities on page 158. Finally, monitor their acquisition of making judgments by using the page 158 assessment.

Use the Graphic Organizer:

    Before Reading

✔ During Reading

✔ After Reading

To Play or Not to Play: The Pros and Cons of Computer Games

Most kids like to play computer games. What does the research say about this pastime? Almost everyone agrees that computer games improve eye-hand coordination. One study even says that surgeons who play computer games make fewer errors than those who don't. Players learn to think quickly. They learn to look for patterns that help them remember complex tasks. They learn to choose the best options. They learn to set and reach goals. They also gain valuable keyboarding skills.

However, experts also agree that computer games can cause problems. The games are expensive. Many are violent. Some players become so used to the quick-moving action that they have trouble following step-by-step directions in the classroom. Some begin to neglect their homework, chores, family, and friends. They miss opportunities to become involved in other fun activities such as hobbies, sports, art, and music.

How do you decide what's best for you? Think about your likes and dislikes. Think about what you do well and what skills you'd like to improve. Think about your family's finances, schedule, and beliefs. Then, with your family's help, make an informed choice. Decide how much computer game time is right for you. In other words, enjoy yourself—but don't let your life become one big game.

Reading Selection Title   To Play or Not to Play: The Pros and Cons of Computer Games

As you read, record judgments about the topic, author, and information. When possible, include opinions, beliefs, or preferences that lead you to take action or make personal choices based on what you read.

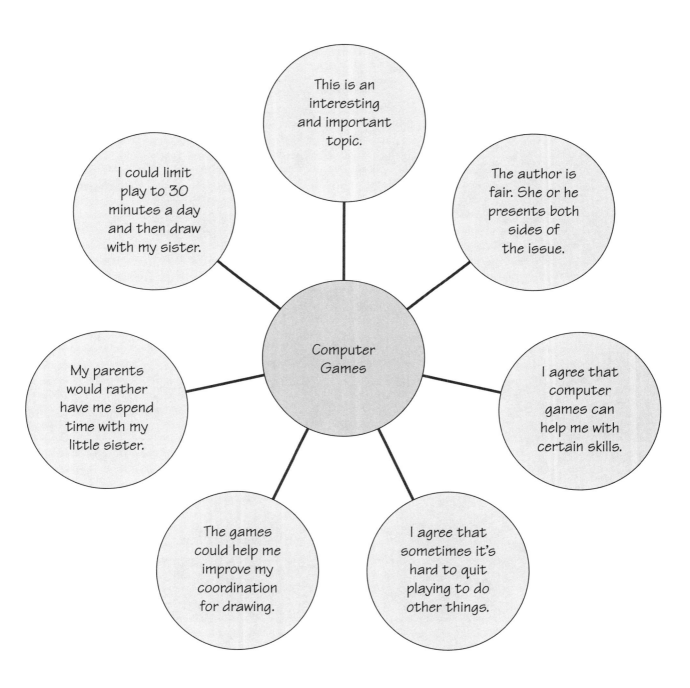

Now use your graphic organizer to summarize the reading selection to a partner.

Name _____ **Date** _____

Reading Selection Title _____

As you read, record judgments about the topic, author, and information. When possible, include opinions, beliefs, or preferences that lead you to take action or make personal choices based on what you read.

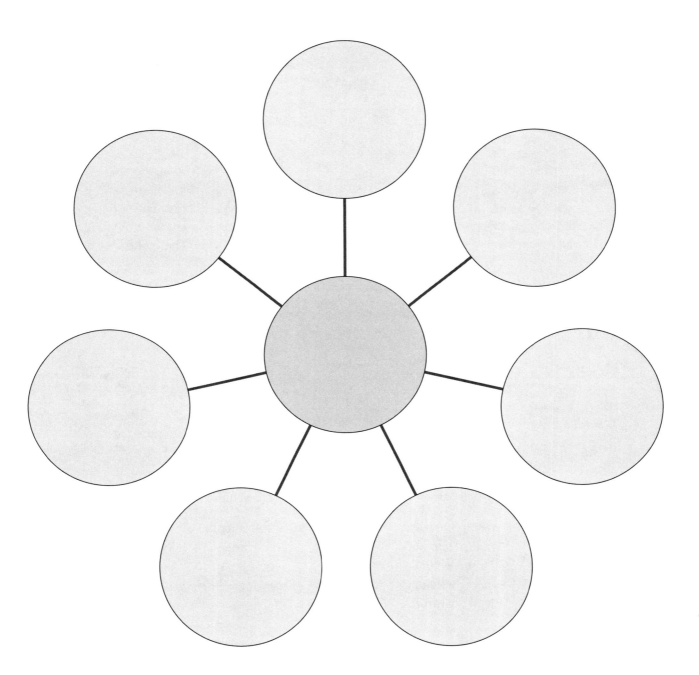

Now use your graphic organizer to summarize the reading selection to a partner.

Name _____   **Date** _____

Use the graphic organizer to make judgments about something you've studied in math, science, or social studies. Then write a paragraph about it.

_____

_____

_____

_____

_____

_____

_____

_____

_____

_____

_____

_____

_____

_____

Sample Topics:

Math: most important way you use math in daily life and why

Science: the electronic device that has most benefited humans and why

Social Studies: the country you'd most like to visit and why

Extension Activities

Have students:

- discuss whether their beliefs or opinions about playing computer games have changed since reading the article and why.

- read brief newspaper articles aloud and then share their judgments about the topic or information.

- share examples of judgments made on information from content-area textbooks.

- use the graphic organizer to make judgments about a content-area video viewed in class.

- use the graphic organizer to make judgments about a famous art reproduction, photograph, or sculpture.

- use the graphic organizer to help make a decision about a class activity, such as a field trip destination or a volunteer project.

Strategy Assessment

Have students sketch their own making judgments graphic organizers on notebook paper. Locate a brief, interesting article. Read it aloud slowly, pausing periodically so students can record information on their graphic organizers. If needed, read it once more at a quicker pace so students can check their work.

Conduct one-on-one or small-group conferences to review students' graphic organizers, clarify any confusion, and answer any questions they still have about the strategy. Use this information to plan additional instruction, if needed, along with opportunities for periodic review and practice.

Connecting with Information and Ideas

Personal experiences, prior knowledge, and other resources readers have used can help them get the most out of a new text. *I helped my sister train our dog—I see how training dolphins could be similar in some ways. We studied early river civilizations in social studies class—I already know a lot about Mesopotamia. I watched a documentary about holidays around the world—people in almost every country celebrate birthdays.* These connections help the reader engage with the information in such a way that the task is more enjoyable, the main ideas are easier to understand, and the facts are simpler to remember.

Introduce the Strategy

Write the word *collecting* on the board. Divide the class into small groups. First, have the groups discuss their personal experiences with collecting objects such as rocks, stamps, or sports cards. Then have them tell what they know about people who collect items as part of their work, such as art gallery owners and scientists. Next, have the students share other resources they know of that mention collections, such as books, magazines, newspapers, television shows, or movies. Finally, ask them to talk about how each of these connections could better help them understand a text they might read about collecting.

Model

Read "Thunderstorm!" on page 160 aloud. Then model how to complete the accompanying graphic organizer (page 161) and use it to summarize the reading selection.

Practice

Have students use a copy of the blank graphic organizer on page 162 to make connections in other nonfiction texts, assisting as needed.

Extend and Assess

Have students complete the related writing assignment on page 163 and one or more of the extension activities on page 164. Finally, monitor their acquisition of making connections by using the page 164 assessment.

Use the Graphic Organizer:

Before Reading

During Reading

✔ After Reading

Thunderstorm!

On a warm day, water from lakes and rivers evaporates into the air. The light, warm air quickly rises, allowing colder air to drop. As the vapors cool, they turn back into water. Then we have rain. All this motion along with wind can cause a storm.

Unless you live where the temperature is always below freezing, you've experienced a thunderstorm. You can see these storms coming by looking at the clouds. Storm clouds are tall and dark. They swirl and grow. Sooner or later, rain begins to fall.

Along with rain, thunderstorms bring lightning and thunder. Lightning is static electricity. Have you ever dragged your feet across a carpet and then touched your finger to another person? You both felt a small shock, didn't you? That's static electricity, too.

In a storm, lightning quickly heats the surrounding air. As a result, it suddenly takes up more space. Just as quickly, the air cools off. That's when you hear a loud crash of thunder.

Have you heard the saying *Lightning never strikes the same place twice?* Don't believe it! In a storm, the tallest "target" will most likely be hit. For example, the Empire State Building in New York City is struck by lightning more than twenty times each year.

Reading Selection Title ___Thunderstorm!___

Record connections between the topic and your personal experiences, prior knowledge, and other resources you have used.

TOPIC: thunderstorms

Personal Experiences:

I've seen many thunderstorms. Once we were driving on the highway during a thunderstorm and could barely see where we were going. We had to pull in to a gas station and wait until the storm was over. When I was little, I was afraid of thunder and lightning and hid under my bed during storms. My uncle lives on a farm and has lightning rods on his barn.

Prior Knowledge:

I've learned to recognize storm clouds when I see them. I knew that warm air rises and cold air drops because the floor is the coldest spot in my bedroom. I learned about static electricity in science class when we rubbed balloons on our hair and then stuck them to the wall. I found out that one reason we use fabric softener on our clothes is to keep them from having static electricity and sticking to each other.

Other Resources:

My mom reads the weather forecast aloud from the newspaper every morning while we eat breakfast. This helps us plan what to wear and whether we need to change any plans for the day. We also watch the weather on TV in the evenings. I've seen several movies about storms, like *Twister* with Bill Paxton and Helen Hunt. I just finished reading *Out of the Dust* by Karen Hesse. It's a fiction book but it tells what life was like in the Dust Bowl when people wanted a thunderstorm.

Now use your graphic organizer to summarize the reading selection to a partner.

Name _____   **Date** _____

Reading Selection Title _____

Record connections between the topic and your personal experiences, prior knowledge, and other resources you have used.

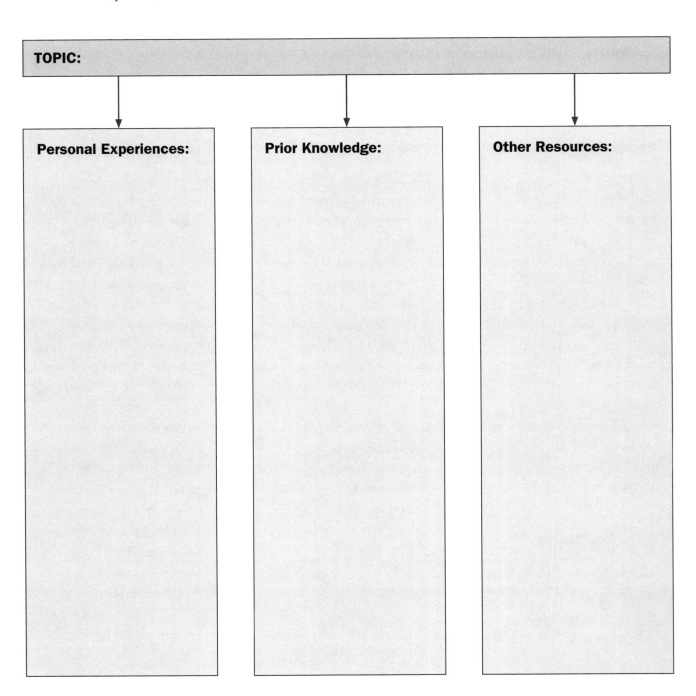

TOPIC:

Personal Experiences:

Prior Knowledge:

Other Resources:

Now use your graphic organizer to summarize the reading selection to a partner.

Name _____   **Date** _____

Use the graphic organizer to make connections to a topic studied in math, science, or social studies. Then write a paragraph about it.

_____

_____

_____

_____

_____

_____

_____

_____

_____

_____

_____

_____

_____

_____

_____

Sample Topics:

Math: the U.S. Mint

Science: the human skeletal system

Social Studies: Rosa Parks

Extension Activities

Have students:

- use the graphic organizer to make connections to an article about another type of weather system.

- share examples of books or other reading selections to which they've had difficulty connecting and explain why.

- share personal experience, prior knowledge, and other resource connections to topics in their content-area textbooks.

- use the graphic organizer to make connections to a documentary viewed in class.

- make a collage of interesting newspaper headlines and share it with the class along with connections they can make with the topics.

- share their connections lists with the class to encourage other students to read particular nonfiction articles or books.

Strategy Assessment

Have students sketch their own connections graphic organizers on notebook paper. Locate a brief, interesting article. Read it aloud slowly, pausing periodically so students can record information on their graphic organizers. If needed, read it once more at a quicker pace so students can check their work.

Conduct one-on-one or small-group conferences to review students' graphic organizers, clarify any confusion, and answer any questions they still have about the strategy. Use this information to plan additional instruction, if needed, along with opportunities for periodic review and practice.

Word Study Units

Finding Meaning— Prefixes and Suffixes

We all like to experience *comfort*. When we do, we feel *comfortable*. When we don't, we sense *discomfort*. Obviously, each of these words is related. *Comfort* is the common word. We can add certain groups of letters to the beginning of the word, called prefixes, to change its meaning. We can add certain groups of letters to the end of the word, called suffixes, to change its meaning in a new way. We can even add both prefixes and suffixes to give the word yet another meaning. (Have you ever had to sit *uncomfortably* close to another person in an airplane?) Effective readers use prefixes and suffixes as a valuable decoding and comprehension tool when reading fiction and nonfiction texts.

Introduce the Strategy

Write the following words on the board and have volunteers use them in oral sentences: (Prefixes) anti*social*, dis*agree*, ex-*president*, im*mature*, in*visible*, micro*scope*, mis*count*, non*stop*, over*priced*, re*write*, sub*zero*, un*happy*, under*paid;* (Suffixes) *learn*able, *teach*er, *fright*en, *quick*er, *host*ess, *soft*est, *cheer*ful, *child*ish, *thought*less, *life*like, *mother*ly, *develop*ment, *dark*ness, *friend*ship. After each sentence, revisit the word and underline the prefix or suffix. Then ask how the sentence would need to be reworded if the prefix or suffix was removed.

Model

Read "Touching Solid Ground" on page 168 aloud. Then model how to complete the accompanying graphic organizer (page 169) and use it to summarize the reading selection.

Practice

Have students use a copy of the blank graphic organizer on page 170 to find words with prefixes and suffixes in other nonfiction or fiction texts, assisting as needed.

Extend and Assess

Have students complete the related writing assignment on page 171 and one or more of the extension activities on page 172. Finally, monitor their acquisition of using prefixes and suffixes to find meaning by using the page 172 assessment.

Use the Graphic Organizer:

Before Reading

✔ During Reading

✔ After Reading

Touching Solid Ground

The rock climber hung dangerously high above the crowd. No one knew what had happened. A minute ago everything seemed fine, but something had gone wrong.

"Wow, I never knew the climbing demonstration would be this exciting," said Paul. "I wonder if Ms. Turner is okay? It looks like her rope is caught in that slider-gadget."

The onlookers held their breath as the stranded climber gently tugged and pulled at the mechanism. She was close to the top of the cliff, so a rescue would be difficult.

After what seemed like hours, the suspended woman began to descend. Everyone clapped loudly. As Ms. Turner reached the ground unharmed, the crowd burst into cheers.

"Well, Paul, do you still want to be a climber after watching my misadventure?" Ms. Turner asked, still shaking a bit from her efforts.

"Even more!" answered Paul. "Now I know that when a problem arises, a climber with skill and patience can solve it. But I'm sure I'll always be relieved to touch solid ground again."

"Yes, you will," laughed Ms. Turner. "I'm plenty relieved myself right now!"

Reading Selection Title ___Touching Solid Ground___

Record words that have prefixes and suffixes. Underline the letters that have been added to the word to change its meaning.

Words with Prefixes	Words with Suffixes	Possible Meanings
	climb<u>er</u>	someone who climbs
	danger<u>ously</u> (ous & ly)	full of danger
	happen<u>ed</u>	past tense of happen
	climb<u>ing</u>	taking a climb
	demonstra<u>tion</u>	something you demonstrate
	excit<u>ing</u>	full of excitement
<u>on</u>lookers	onlook<u>ers</u>	people who look on or watch
	gent<u>ly</u>	being gentle
	tugg<u>ed</u>	past tense of tug
	pull<u>ed</u>	past tense of pull
	seem<u>ed</u>	past tense of seem
	suspend<u>ed</u>	past tense of suspend
<u>de</u>scend		move downward
	clapp<u>ed</u>	past tense of clap
	loud<u>ly</u>	sounding loud
<u>un</u>harmed	unharm<u>ed</u>	not receiving harm
	watch<u>ing</u>	getting to watch
<u>mis</u>adventure		adventure that went bad
	ask<u>ed</u>	past tense of ask
	shak<u>ing</u>	having the shakes
	answer<u>ed</u>	past tense of answer
	reliev<u>ed</u>	past tense of relieve
	laugh<u>ed</u>	past tense of laugh

Now use your graphic organizer to summarize the reading selection to a partner.

Name _____   **Date** _____

Reading Selection Title _____

Record words that have prefixes and suffixes. Underline the letters that have been added to the word to change its meaning.

Words with Prefixes	Words with Suffixes	Possible Meanings

Now use your graphic organizer to summarize the reading selection to a partner.

Name _____   **Date** _____

Read a brief fiction or nonfiction selection and use the graphic organizer to record words with prefixes and suffixes. Then write a paragraph using at least two of the words.

_____

_____

_____

_____

_____

_____

_____

_____

_____

_____

_____

_____

_____

_____

_____

_____

Extension Activities

Have students:

- use the graphic organizer to locate prefixes and suffixes in a story or article about another extreme sport.

- create a classroom reference chart listing the meanings of common prefixes and suffixes along with several examples of each.

- locate and share words with prefixes and suffixes from their content-area textbooks.

- use a highlighter to mark words with prefixes and suffixes in a newspaper article.

- play a game in which one student calls out a word and the others try to think of versions of the word that include prefixes and suffixes, such as: *list—listed, listing, unlisted, enlist, re-enlist* or *kind—unkind, kindly, kindness, unkindness, kinder, kindest.*

- sort words into categories. For example, the following underlined prefixes and suffixes all indicate size: (large) *macroeconomics, magnificent, megawatt;* (half) *hemisphere;* and (small) *microscope, dinette, duckling, cubicle, molecule, starlet.*

Strategy Assessment

As students sketch their own prefix/suffix graphic organizers on notebook paper, write the following statements on the board. Have students analyze them and record the results on their graphic organizers.

- Explorers climbing extremely high mountains may encounter ice.

- Ice climbers need special equipment, such as attachable boot spikes.

- Inexperienced mountaineers should not try ascending ice walls.

Conduct one-on-one or small-group conferences to review students' graphic organizers, clarify any confusion, and answer any questions they still have about the strategy. Use this information to plan additional instruction, if needed, along with opportunities for periodic review and practice.

Finding Meaning—Homographs

You see a fan. Is a device stirring up the air or is someone admiring you? You see a bass. Are you fishing or watching a choir perform? The words *fan/fan* and *bass/bass* are homographs— words that are spelled the same but have different meanings and different origins. Some homographs have the same pronunciation, such as *fan* and *fan*, but others are pronounced differently, such as *bass* and *bass*. When looking up a homograph in the dictionary, readers will see different entries for each version of the word and must be sure to choose the one that makes sense in the text.

Introduce the Strategy

Assign each student a partner, and give each pair a homograph written on a slip of paper. Have each partner act out a different meaning of the word while the class tries to guess what it is. For example, for the word *bat*, one student might pretend to fly while the other pretends to hit a baseball. Continue until all students have had a turn and then discuss the homographs they have pantomimed. Following are some sample homographs and meaning clues. (Those that are pronounced differently are underlined.):

bow	(ribbon/greeting)
box	(container/sport)
close	(shut/near)
crow	(rooster call/black bird)
desert	(dry region/leave)
dove	(bird/did dive)
felt	(touched/soft cloth)
hide	(keep out of sight/animal skin)
jerky	(uneven movements/dried meat)
lead	(show the way/tip of pencil)
lie	(falsehood/rest)
loaf	(goof off/bread)
object	(complain/item)
palm	(inside of hand/tree)

pen	(tool for writing/enclosed area)
pitcher	(container for liquids/baseball player)
pound	(sixteen ounces/hit hard)
present	(to introduce/gift)
punch	(hit/beverage)
pupil	(student/center of eye)
racket	(noise/tennis tool)
rare	(unusual/barely cooked)
record	(write down/document)
refuse	(say no/trash)
row	(line/using oars)
saw	(did see/cutting tool)
sow	(scatter seeds/female pig)
squash	(vegetable/press flat)
stick	(piece of wood/pierce)
tear	(liquid from eye/pull apart)
tire	(become weary/rubber on wheel),
well	(satisfactory/hole dug for water)
wind	(moving air/turn)

Model

Read "Good News Night" on page 174 aloud. Then model how to complete the accompanying graphic organizer (page 175) and use it to summarize the reading selection.

Practice

Have students use a copy of the blank graphic organizer on page 176 to find homographs in other nonfiction or fiction texts, assisting as needed.

Extend and Assess

Have students complete the related writing assignment on page 177 and one or more of the extension activities on page 178. Finally, monitor their acquisition of using homographs to find meaning by using the page 178 assessment.

Use the Graphic Organizer:

Before Reading

✔ During Reading

✔ After Reading

Good News Night

"It's Friday—Good News Night," Dad said as he carried a bowl of spaghetti into the dining room. "Who wants to go first?"

"Pasghetti for supper is good news," said Frankie, holding out his plate.

"Frankie learning to say 'spaghetti' would be good news," said Carla as she passed a basket of garlic bread around the table.

"Come on, you know what I mean," said Dad. "What happened this week that made you excited or content? I can think of lots of things! Bo finally learned not to bark at the mail carrier when she comes into the yard. I got the bills paid with enough money left over to take you two to the fair tomorrow. And to top it all off, the local radio station read a clip from my newspaper column on the air. It's been a great week!"

"Congrats, Dad!" said Carla. "Let's see . . . I found my missing birthstone ring under my bed. I lowered my time at swim team practice by three seconds per lap. Oh yeah . . . I also got the top score in the class on my math test."

"Way to go!" said Dad. "Your turn, Frankie."

"Well . . . I learned to count to 100 at kindergarten—except for some of the seventies and eighties. I learned to tell which is my left hand and which is my right—unless I'm standing on my head. And . . . and . . . I didn't get chased by a bear!"

Dad laughed and ruffled Frankie's hair. "That's great, son!" he said.

"Good News Night is certainly never boring!" said Carla, smiling. "Any more pasghetti, anyone?"

Reading Selection Title ___Good News Night___

Record homographs from the reading selection. Show how they are used in the story. Then create sentences that show another use of each homograph.

Word	Story Sentence	Sentence with Homograph
bowl	Dad put a bowl of spaghetti on the dinner table.	My uncle likes to bowl every Tuesday night with his buddies.
table	Carla passed a basket of garlic bread around the table.	The average rainfall is included on the weather table in the newspaper.
content	What made you excited or content?	The content of the documentary was too complicated for young children.
bark	Bo learned not to bark at the mail carrier . . .	The woodpecker chipped away at the tree bark looking for insects to eat.
yard	when she comes into the yard.	I used one yard of fabric to make the pillow on the sofa.
bills	I got the bills paid . . .	Birds' bills come in many shapes, sizes, and colors.
fair	with enough money to take you two to the fair tomorrow.	I'm only a fair soccer player, but I excel at basketball.
clip	The local radio station read a clip from my newspaper column.	Clip these papers together before putting them in the file cabinet.
ring	I found my missing birthstone ring.	Grandma will ring the bell on the porch when breakfast is ready.
seconds	I lowered my time at swim team practice by three seconds . . .	This cake is delicious. May I have seconds?
lap	per lap.	The baby sat quietly in his mother's lap.
top	I got the top score in the class on my math test.	The spinning top flew off the table and onto the floor.
count	I learned to count to 100.	The count commanded his subjects to pay taxes on their farm animals.
left	I learned to tell which is my left hand.	We left school as soon as the final bell rang.
bear	I didn't get chased by a bear.	I don't think this flimsy shelf can bear the weight of all those books.
ruffled	Dad ruffled Frankie's hair.	The ruffled blouse will go perfectly with this skirt.
boring	"Good News Night" is certainly never boring.	The carpenter is boring holes in the wood before attaching the sections.

Now use your graphic organizer to summarize the reading selection to a partner.

Name _____ **Date** _____

Reading Selection Title _____

Record homographs from the reading selection. Show how they are used in the story. Then create sentences that show another use of each homograph.

Word	Story Sentence	Sentence with Homograph

Now use your graphic organizer to summarize the reading selection to a partner.

Name _____ **Date** _____

Read a brief fiction or nonfiction selection and use the graphic organizer to record homographs.
Then write a paragraph using at least two of the words in more than one way.

_____

_____

_____

_____

_____

_____

_____

_____

_____

_____

_____

_____

_____

_____

_____

Extension Activities

Have students:

- repeat the "Introduce the Strategy" activity with different homographs.

- write their own lists of good news items using as many homographs as possible.

- locate and share examples of homographs from their content-area textbooks.

- explore several homographs in the dictionary and see who can find the one with the most entries.

- play a game in which a student says two sentences using a homograph but leaves out the word. The rest of the class then tries to guess the missing word, such as *My big brother told a funny (blank). The elevator broke down on the fourth (blank) of the building.* (Answer: *story*)

- make a booklet that includes drawings of various homographs, such as a *school* where classes are held and a *school* of fish or a *bank* where you can deposit money and a river *bank*.

Strategy Assessment

As students sketch their own homograph graphic organizers on notebook paper, write some or all of the following statements on the board. Have students analyze them and record the results on their graphic organizers.

- "Don't forget to *duck* when you go under the tree branch," said Dad.

- "I wish I could *fly* over the branches," said Frankie.

- "Hiking is *fine* with me," said Carla.

- "Your *gum* is swollen," said the dentist.

- "You'll need a *light* jacket for the field trip," said Mr. Berl.

- "May I have the *rest* of the cereal?" Krissy asked.

- "Mom always leaves a nice *tip* for the waitress," Hunter said.

Conduct one-on-one or small-group conferences to review students' graphic organizers, clarify any confusion, and answer any questions they still have about the strategy. Use this information to plan additional instruction, if needed, along with opportunities for periodic review and practice.

Finding Meaning— Synonyms and Antonyms

Synonyms are words that have the same or similar meaning, such as *hurry* and *rush.* Antonyms are words that have opposite meanings, such as *failure* and *success.* Effective readers use synonyms and antonyms in a text to help them figure out tricky words. For example, the author might say *Some birds construct, or build, their nests from mud* or *The shopkeeper was always busy— never idle.* Other times readers can check their understanding by mentally inserting a synonym or antonym into a sentence to see if it makes sense. Both a dictionary and a thesaurus are valuable tools for readers working with synonyms and antonyms.

Introduce the Strategy

Give each student two index cards. Have them write the letter S on one card and the letter A on the other. Tell them you will say a pair of words, such as *take / grab.* If the words' meanings are similar, students should hold up the **S** card for *synonym.* If the words have opposite meanings, students should hold up the **A** card for *antonyms.* Use some or all of the following:

say / state (S)	*copy / original* (A)
above / below (A)	*walk / stroll* (S)
finish / start (A)	*exceptional / common* (A)
wealth / riches (S)	*fresh / stale* (A)
write / record (S)	*repair / destroy* (A)
expand / shrink (A)	*play / frolic* (S)
world / earth (S)	*marvelous / wonderful* (S)
look / glance (S)	*temporary / permanent* (A)
capture / release (A)	

Model

Read "Creatures of the Desert" on page 180 aloud. Then model how to complete the accompanying graphic organizer (page 181) and use it to summarize the reading selection.

Practice

Have students use a copy of the blank graphic organizer on page 182 to find synonyms and antonyms in other nonfiction or fiction texts, assisting as needed.

Extend and Assess

Have students complete the related writing assignment on page 183 and one or more of the extension activities on page 184. Finally, monitor their acquisition of using synonyms and antonyms to find meaning by using the page 184 assessment.

Use the Graphic Organizer:

Before Reading
✔ During Reading
✔ After Reading

Creatures of the Desert

The red-orange sun setting over the North American desert brings out creatures large and small. You may see squirrels, mice, bats, foxes, rabbits, and deer. You may see snakes, tortoises, horned toads, and gila monsters. You may see cactus wrens, roadrunners, owls, sparrows, and hawks. You may even see spiders, scorpions, termites, and beetles.

To find many of these creatures, look in, under, and around the giant saguaro cacti. Their fleshy, or plump, green stems store water. Their fruit and nectar provide food for the animals.

Tiny birds and insects often stay inside the saguaro during the heat of the day. When the temperature begins to cool, they move outside to search for food. However, sometimes they become food for other creatures. For example, rodents seek insects, snakes look for rodents, and desert owls hunt for snakes.

All the creatures of the desert depend on each other . . . and on the saguaros.

From *Show Me!,* Copyright © Good Year Books. This page may be reproduced for classroom use only by the actual purchaser of the book. www.goodyearbooks.com

Reading Selection Title   Creatures of the Desert

Record words that have synonyms and antonyms. Write examples from the text and examples you know. If you can't think of anything, try a dictionary or thesaurus.

Word	Synonym in Text	Synonym I Know	Antonym in Text	Antonym I Know
over		above	under	
North				South
out			in	
creatures	animals			
large	giant	big, huge	small, tiny	little
find		discover, locate		lose
many		lots, several		few
fleshy	plump			thin, skinny
store		keep, save, collect		
provide		give, offer, supply		
often		frequently		never
stay				leave, depart
inside		within	outside	
heat		warmth	cool	cold
day		daytime		night
begins		starts		ends
search	look, seek, hunt			
sometimes		occasionally		never
food		provisions		
depend on		need, require		

Now use your graphic organizer to summarize the reading selection to a partner.

Name _____ **Date** _____

Reading Selection Title _____

Record words that have synonyms and antonyms. Write examples from the text and examples you know. If you can't think of anything, try a dictionary or thesaurus.

Word	Synonym in Text	Synonym I Know	Antonym in Text	Antonym I Know

Now use your graphic organizer to summarize the reading selection to a partner.

Name _____ **Date** _____

Read a brief fiction or nonfiction selection and use the graphic organizer to record synonyms and antonyms. Then write a paragraph using at least two of the word pairs.

_____

_____

_____

_____

_____

_____

_____

_____

_____

_____

_____

_____

_____

_____

_____

Extension Activities

Have students:

- use the graphic organizer to record synonyms and antonyms from another story or article about the desert.

- repeat the "Introduce the Strategy" activity using new synonym and antonym pairs.

- locate and share synonyms and antonyms from their content-area textbooks.

- keep a log of new words encountered in their independent reading, and use a dictionary and thesaurus to locate applicable synonyms and antonyms.

- make up "silly sentences" by replacing words with their antonyms and have the rest of the class figure out how to fix them, such as *The bread was fresh so I threw it out* (The bread was *stale*) or *My brother is so stingy that he let me ride his new bike* (My brother was *generous*).

- divide into teams, give each team member a thesaurus, take turns calling out a word, and see who can find the most synonyms and/or antonyms in a designated period of time.

Strategy Assessment

As students sketch their own synonym/antonym graphic organizers on notebook paper, write the following statements on the board. Have students analyze them and record the results on their graphic organizers.

- A young saguaro may be as short as your pencil, but an old one may be as tall as a three-story building.

- Saguaros have spines, not leaves, so they don't lose as much water as trees do.

- A saguaro may look plain, but on summer nights its flowers open and provide a fancy décor, or design.

Conduct one-on-one or small-group conferences to review students' graphic organizers, clarify any confusion, and answer any questions they still have about the strategy. Use this information to plan additional instruction, if needed, along with opportunities for periodic review and practice.

Finding Meaning—Context Clues

Although the dictionary is an invaluable invention, most people don't enjoy interrupting their reading to look up new words. Good readers learn to use other words in a sentence or other sentences in a paragraph to figure out what a tricky word means. Authors provide several types of context clues. Sometimes they directly define a word using phrases such as *is called* or *which means* or punctuation such as commas, dashes, or parentheses. Often they use synonyms or antonyms to help define the word. Other times they indirectly support the word by describing it, placing it in a category, or providing an example.

Introduce the Strategy

Have students use their dictionaries to locate little-known words and then write a sentence for each one that give clues to its meaning. As they read their sentences aloud, have the rest of the class try to determine the meaning of the word based on the clues. Discuss the techniques students use and record them on the chalkboard, such as:

- using the phrase *are called*
- using a comma or dash followed by an explanation of the word
- defining the word in parentheses
- using a synonym
- using an antonym
- describing the word
- putting the word into a familiar category
- giving one or more examples of the word

Model

Read "Goalie of the Year" on page 186 aloud. Then model how to complete the accompanying graphic organizer (page 187) and use it to summarize the reading selection.

Practice

Have students use a copy of the blank graphic organizer on page 188 to find context clues in other nonfiction or fiction texts, assisting as needed.

Extend and Assess

Have students complete the related writing assignment on page 189 and one or more of the extension activities on page 190. Finally, monitor their acquisition of using context clues to find meaning by using the page 190 assessment.

Use the Graphic Organizer:

Before Reading

✔ During Reading

After Reading

Goalie of the Year

"Your save won the game!" exclaimed Kris, slapping Stefan on the back. "You're sure to be named Goalie of the Year!"

"I think you should be Goalie of the Decade!" said Susan. "The Soccer League will be lucky to have another player like you in the next ten years."

"Why settle for a decade?" asked Kris. "Let's go for Goalie of the Century!"

"One hundred years?" laughed Stefan. "I won't even be around to see who takes my place!"

"In that case, why not make it a millennium—a thousand years?" asked Susan.

"Speaking of time, I learned something new in science class," said Stefan. "The sun takes a cosmic year, which is about 225 million of our years, to revolve around the center of the Milky Way."

"Wow!" said Kris. "I wonder if people will even know what soccer is by then? I guess Goalie of the Year sounds pretty good after all."

"Yes," said Stefan. "I'd be proud to earn the annual award. But whether I do or not, I'll always remember this year's soccer season."

Reading Selection Title _Goalie of the Year_

Record new words you find in the reading selection. Then record the context clues that help you figure out the meaning of each word.

Word	Context Clues
goalie	save won the soccer game
decade	the next ten years
League	soccer another player
settle	Why . . . ? Let's go for . . .
century	one hundred years
millennium	a thousand years
cosmic year	about 225 million of our years
Milky Way	sun revolves around the center
annual	this year's soccer season

Now use your graphic organizer to summarize the reading selection to a partner.

Name _____   **Date** _____

Reading Selection Title _____

Record new words you find in the reading selection. Then record the context clues that help you figure out the meaning of each word.

Word	Context Clues

Now use your graphic organizer to summarize the reading selection to a partner.

Name _____   **Date** _____

Read a brief fiction or nonfiction selection and use the graphic organizer to record new words and their context clues. Then write a paragraph using at least two of the words.

_____

_____

_____

_____

_____

_____

_____

_____

_____

_____

_____

_____

_____

_____

_____

_____

Extension Activities

Have students:

- repeat the "Introduce the Strategy" activity using new words.

- highlight context clue techniques used in newspaper articles.

- locate and share examples of context clues from their content-area textbooks.

- locate and share examples of photographs and illustrations that provide meaning clues for fiction and nonfiction reading selections.

- locate book titles that use subtitles to help explain their meanings, such as *The Tale of Despereaux: Being the Story of a Mouse, A Princess, Some Soup, and a Spool of Thread* by Kate Dicamillo or *The Everything Kids' Science Experiments Book: Boil Ice, Float Water, Measure Gravity—Challenge the World Around You!* by Tom Robinson.

- use the graphic organizer to record context clues they hear in your current classroom read-aloud.

Strategy Assessment

As students sketch their own context clues graphic organizers on notebook paper, write some or all of the following statements on the board. Have students analyze them and record the results on their graphic organizers.

- Soccer, an outdoor ball and goal game, is called football or association football in some countries. It differs from rugby, where players may kick, carry, or pass the ball. American football is a version, or type, of rugby.

- Soccer is the most popular team sport internationally. Americans prefer their own version of football but have soccer teams from preschool through professional level (Major League Soccer).

- Billions of people watch the biggest quadrennial soccer tournament ever—the World Cup—on television every four years as national teams seek to be named champions of the world.

Conduct one-on-one or small-group conferences to review students' graphic organizers, clarify any confusion, and answer any questions they still have about the strategy. Use this information to plan additional instruction, if needed, along with opportunities for periodic review and practice.

Descriptive Language— Similes and Metaphors

Similes are figures of speech that describe by comparing two objects, places, people, or actions using the word *like* or *as*. Some common similes are *as sweet as honey, fits like a glove, as comfortable as an old shoe, runs like the wind,* and *as busy as a bee.* Metaphors, on the other hand, indirectly compare by claiming something IS something else. For example, you use metaphor when you call someone a *walking encyclopedia,* a *couch potato,* a *bottomless pit,* or a *clinging vine.* Both similes and metaphors are used in place of adjectives and adverbs to help readers picture or visualize a particular idea.

Introduce the Strategy

Have students sketch an object in their homes and then describe it in as many ways as possible. Most will start with adjectives, but encourage them to compare the object to other familiar things as well. To model, sketch a picture of a sofa on the chalkboard. Beside the sketch, make a list of words and phrases such as *long, has blue paisley fabric, has cushions, has a pull-out bed inside, has a ketchup stain on the arm.* Next, write some similes, such as *soft as a cloud, heavy as an elephant,* or *helps me sleep like a baby.* Finally, add some metaphors, such as *an island in a sea of carpet, an old friend,* or *a safe haven after a busy day.* After students complete their sketches and lists, have them share with the class. Record and discuss any similes or metaphors they include.

Model

Read "The Old Mill" on page 192 aloud. Then model how to complete the accompanying graphic organizer (page 193) and use it to summarize the reading selection.

Practice

Have students use a copy of the blank graphic organizer on page 194 to find similes and metaphors in other nonfiction or fiction texts, assisting as needed.

Extend and Assess

Have students complete the related writing assignment on page 195 and one or more of the extension activities on page 196. Finally, monitor their acquisition of using similes and metaphors to describe by using the page 196 assessment.

Use the Graphic Organizer:

Before Reading

✔ During Reading

✔ After Reading

The Old Mill

The massive building with its dried oatmeal paint sat alone, hidden by overgrowth. The faded red roof, once a bed of roses beckoning onlookers from miles away, sagged its shoulders. The stream trickled by like a leaky faucet, plunking a lonely melody of yesteryear. The retaining wall soldiers stood tall and watchful, covered in an ivy blanket.

"What is this place, Dad?" asked Theo. "We've never hiked here when we visited Grandma and Granddad before."

"It's a mill," said Dad. "Once people came from far and wide to buy flour for baking. Remember the cloth sacks Grandma has framed on her kitchen wall? Those came from this very mill."

"It's a cool building. It's too bad someone doesn't do something with it," remarked Theo.

"That's why I brought you here," said Dad. "I've bought this place. We're moving back here and opening a restaurant inside the mill. It'll be a lot of work, but people will come from all the nearby villages. I'll bet some of our friends in the city will even make the drive!"

"Wow—a restaurant!" exclaimed Theo. "Can I help after school and in the summers?"

"Sure," said Dad. "I was hoping you would. I'd also like you to name the restaurant. All I can think of is 'The Old Mill,' but that's not catchy enough."

"How about 'The Flour Sack'?" asked Theo. "I'll bet we could find some more of those old sacks to frame."

"You're a genius!" said Dad. "The Flour Sack it is. I'm as excited as a kid in a toy shop!"

Reading Selection Title ___The Old Mill___

Record and label similes and metaphors. Then explain them in your own words.

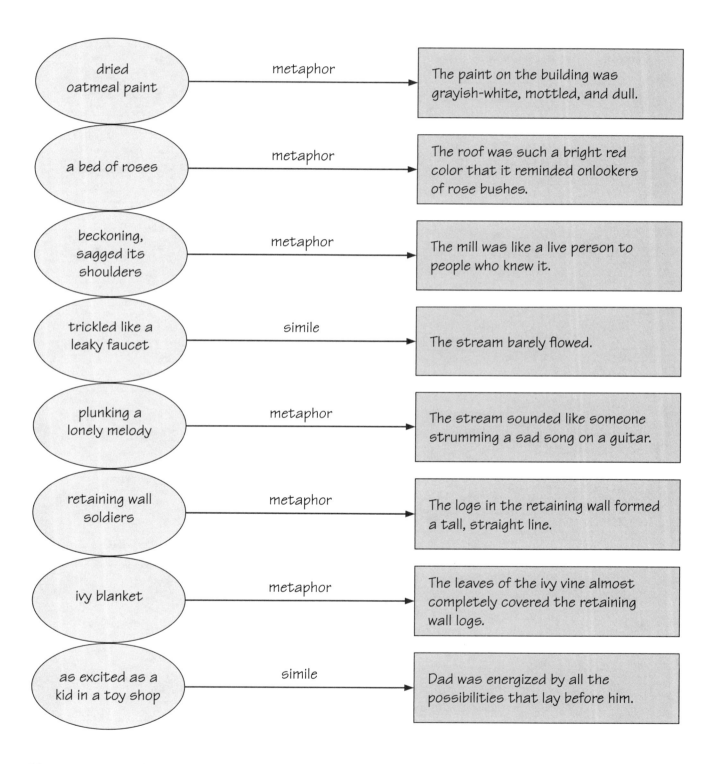

dried oatmeal paint	metaphor	The paint on the building was grayish-white, mottled, and dull.
a bed of roses	metaphor	The roof was such a bright red color that it reminded onlookers of rose bushes.
beckoning, sagged its shoulders	metaphor	The mill was like a live person to people who knew it.
trickled like a leaky faucet	simile	The stream barely flowed.
plunking a lonely melody	metaphor	The stream sounded like someone strumming a sad song on a guitar.
retaining wall soldiers	metaphor	The logs in the retaining wall formed a tall, straight line.
ivy blanket	metaphor	The leaves of the ivy vine almost completely covered the retaining wall logs.
as excited as a kid in a toy shop	simile	Dad was energized by all the possibilities that lay before him.

Now use your graphic organizer to summarize the reading selection to a partner.

Name _____ **Date** _____

Reading Selection Title _____

Record and label similes and metaphors. Then explain them in your own words.

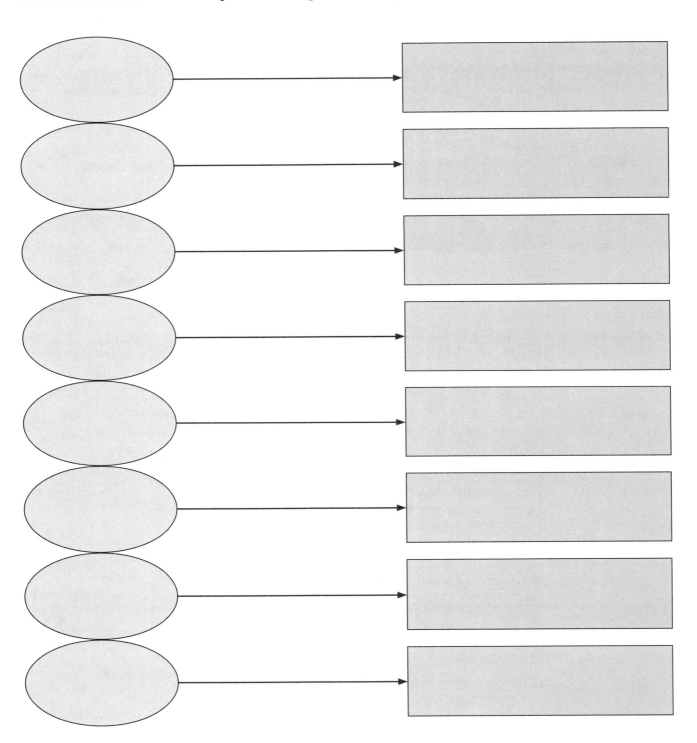

Now use your graphic organizer to summarize the reading selection to a partner.

Name _____ **Date** _____

Read a brief fiction or nonfiction selection and use the graphic organizer to record similes and metaphors. Then write a paragraph using one of the examples.

_____

_____

_____

_____

_____

_____

_____

_____

_____

_____

_____

_____

_____

_____

_____

Extension Activities

Have students:

- rewrite several sentences in the reading selection using new similes and metaphors.

- locate and share poems that include similes and metaphors.

- locate and share examples of similes and metaphors from their content-area textbooks.

- cut out interesting pictures from old newspapers or magazines and describe each one with a simile or metaphor.

- write humorous, pretend radio advertisements for products of their choice in which every sentence contains a simile or metaphor.

- draw literal illustrations for common metaphors, such as *the flowers danced in the breeze* or *the football player was a moose.*

Strategy Assessment

As students sketch their own similes/metaphor graphic organizers on notebook paper, write some or all of the following statements on the board. Have students analyze them and record the results on their graphic organizers.

- Long ago, the old mill was as noisy as a hive of bees.

- Dad kept his idea bottled up inside for a long time.

- Theo was a ping-pong ball bouncing on the ground when he heard Dad's idea.

- The newly painted roof was as red as an apple.

- Dad sent a snail mail letter to all the relatives telling them about his plans.

- News about the restaurant spread like wildfire.

- As quick as a wink, the first customers made reservations.

Conduct one-on-one or small-group conferences to review students' graphic organizers, clarify any confusion, and answer any questions they still have about the strategy. Use this information to plan additional instruction, if needed, along with opportunities for periodic review and practice.

Descriptive Language—Idioms

Shelly was **down in the dumps**, but she didn't **throw in the towel**. Instead, she **pulled some strings** and got picked to be the **big cheese** in the school play. Now she has **butterflies in her stomach**, but I've got it **straight from the horse's mouth** that her performance will **bring down the house!** The bold-faced phrases in the previous scenario are called *idioms*. Idioms are words used in a special way. If taken literally, they create confusing and often humorous pictures in a reader's mind—particularly if English is not his or her native language. To understand idioms, readers must pay close attention to what is happening in the text and use logical thinking to infer their intended meanings.

Introduce the Strategy

Have individuals or small groups of students act out the literal meaning of several idioms. For example, if the idiom is *horsing around*, students will pretend to be horses running in a circle. Then have the rest of the class guess the idiom and discuss its common meaning in the English language. Examples are:

stole the spotlight

put your foot in your mouth

blew her top

drives me up the wall

off the hook

frog in my throat

in the same boat

cat's got your tongue

hit the nail on the head

wake up and smell the coffee

on the right track

head in the clouds

cold feet

fly in the ointment

shed some light on it

under your hat

sitting pretty

put your money where your mouth is

knock your socks off

plays by ear

hot under the collar

pretty kettle of fish

got my goat

Finally, ask students to share idioms they know to add to the list.

Model

Read "The Penny Pincher Book Sale" on page 198 aloud. Then model how to complete the accompanying graphic organizer (page 199) and use it to summarize the reading selection.

Practice

Have students use a copy of the blank graphic organizer on page 200 to find idioms in other nonfiction or fiction texts, assisting as needed.

Extend and Assess

Have students complete the related writing assignment on page 201 and one or more of the extension activities on page 202. Finally, monitor their acquisition of using idioms to describe by using the page 202 assessment.

Use the Graphic Organizer:

Before Reading

✔ During Reading

✔ After Reading

The Penny Pincher Book Sale

"What's the matter, Shay?" asked Kerrie as he joined his friend on the front steps of the apartment building. "Did you get up on the wrong side of the bed?"

"I couldn't wait for summer to come, but now I can't think of anything to do," replied Shay, sighing.

"You're pulling my leg, right?" asked Kerrie. "You've always got something up your sleeve to keep me from turning into a complete bookworm!"

"Books! That's it!" shouted Shay. "Let's organize a book exchange in the courtyard on Saturday. People can bring books they've already read and trade for different ones. It'll be fun, and we'll all have something new to read."

"Great idea, Shay!" said Kerrie. "We can call it the 'Penny Pincher Book Sale' because no one has to spend a cent. I'll try to butter up Mrs. Carson and see if we can borrow some of her big tables. Plus, if I tell her about the sale, we won't have to worry about publicity. She's famous for letting the cat out of the bag!"

A week later, Kerrie again saw Shay sitting on the stoop. "How's it going?" he asked.

"I'm on cloud nine!" said Shay. "I just read the best book. Now I'm passing it on to you, and you don't even have to trade me one. It's on the house!"

"Thanks!" exclaimed Kerrie. "I guess we're BOTH bookworms!"

Reading Selection Title ___The Penny Pincher Book Sale___

Write the idiom. Draw a sketch of what the words mean if taken literally. Then write what the author really means.

Idiom	Literal Sketch	Actual Meaning
get up on the wrong side of the bed		being grouchy for no apparent reason
pulling my leg		kidding or teasing
something up your sleeve		a secret plan
bookworm		someone who reads nearly all the time
penny pincher		someone who doesn't like to spend money
butter up		be nice to someone in order to get him or her to do something nice for you
letting the cat out of the bag		revealing interesting news to other people
on cloud nine		feeling quite happy and contented
on the house		free, no charge

Now use your graphic organizer to summarize the reading selection to a partner.

Name _____ **Date** _____

Reading Selection Title _____

Write the idiom. Draw a sketch of what the words mean if taken literally. Then write what the author really means.

Idiom	Literal Sketch	Actual Meaning

Now use your graphic organizer to summarize the reading selection to a partner.

Name _____   **Date** _____

Read a brief fiction or nonfiction selection and use the graphic organizer to record idioms.
Then write a paragraph using at least two examples.

_____

_____

_____

_____

_____

_____

_____

_____

_____

_____

_____

_____

_____

_____

_____

Extension Activities

Have students:

- repeat the "Introduce the Strategy" activity using different idioms.

- explore books and Web sites on etymology to discover how different idioms got their origins.

- locate and share examples of idioms from their content-area textbooks.

- discuss how "passing on" idioms through generations helps preserve our history, language, and culture.

- write a humorous list of excuses for not turning in their homework that include as many idioms as possible.

- sort idioms into those with positive connotations, such as *a feather in your cap*, and those with negative connotations, such as *a chip on his shoulder*.

Strategy Assessment

As students sketch their own idiom graphic organizers on notebook paper, write some or all of the following statements on the board. Have students analyze them and record the results on their graphic organizers.

- My sister and I have been fighting over closet space for months, but now it's time to bury the hatchet.

- If you think I'm going to lend you the money, you're barking up the wrong tree.

- We'll never make it to school on time if you don't shake a leg!

- I wanted Mom's birthday gift to be a surprise, but you had to go and spill the beans.

- Sean was supposed to help with the science fair project, but he left me high and dry.

- Dad said to be home before noon, so I'd better hit the road.

- I tried to learn how to knit, but I was all thumbs.

- We had to cancel the class field trip because it was raining cats and dogs.

Conduct one-on-one or small-group conferences to review students' graphic organizers, clarify any confusion, and answer any questions they still have about the strategy. Use this information to plan additional instruction, if needed, along with opportunities for periodic review and practice.